Every Harry Potter fan... is left with a sense that there's a lot more to the saga. No worries, leave it to Irvin Khaytman... to present this carefully researched and brilliantly written walk through all seven novels, laying out a very plausible scenario for what Dumbledore knew and when.
—Steve Vander Ark, The Harry Potter Lexicon, *In Search of Harry Potter*

Between his deep understanding of the Harry Potter *series and his excellent writing skills, Irvin's "The Life and Lies of Albus Dumbledore" is a must-read for Harry Potter fans. The book impressively explores the most fascinating character in the series. Get ready to see Dumbledore in a whole new light.*
—Andrew Sims, Hypable.com, MuggleCast

Dumbledore: greatest of teachers or Machiavellian schemer? Irvin Khaytman reconciles these aspects of the character through an investigation of Dumbledore's final years, particularly his last great project: the race to identify and destroy Voldemort's Horcruxes... If your understanding of love, death, and goodness have been influenced by these stories—if you're part of the Harry Potter generation—then this book is for you.
—Lorrie Kim, *SNAPE: A Definitive Reading*

Potterheads rejoice! Longtime Harry Potter fan Irvin Khaytman has provided a deep investigation of all things Albus Dumbledore in his new book... The intense scrutiny provided here helps us see the entirety of Dumbledore's character. Khaytman pays Dumbledore the greatest compliment of all: the proof that he was human after all.
—Cathy Leogrande, Ph.D., Associate Professor of Education, Le Moyne College, Syracuse NY

Irvin Khaytman provides a thorough analysis of Albus Dumbledore's history, intentions, and plans throughout the series. The reading will make you want to reread the series again and allow you to feel a sense of connection with the characters.
—Janina Scarlet, Ph.D., *Harry Potter Therapy: An Unauthorized Self-Help Book from the Restricted Section*

An engaging, in-depth, comprehensive and unique examination of one of J.K. Rowling's most enigmatic stars. Its premise and execution has the polish and power of an academic dissertation while being an extremely accessible, enjoyable read. […] This book is an impetus to engage further with a dynamic, enthusiastic global community who knows that books and love are the most powerful magic of all.
—Leanna Renee Hieber, *Darker Still*, the *Strangely Beautiful* saga

I'd like to venture this might be the most fun you'll ever have reading a book of critical essays. Like Dumbledore himself, this book is both insightful and delightful and written with an abundance of charm, intelligence and a great deal of love for Harry Potter. *I've reread the HP series probably around a dozen times, and this presented me with theories I had never considered before.*
—Sarvenaz Tash, *The Geek's Guide to Unrequited Love*

THE LIFE AND LIES

OF

ALBUS PERCIVAL WULFRIC BRIAN

DUMBLEDORE

Irvin Khaytman

Copyright 2018 by Irvin Khaytman

All rights reserved. No part of this publication may be reproduced, distributed or transmitted in any form or by any means, including photocopying, recording, or other electronic or mechanical methods, without the prior written permission of the author, except in the case of brief quotations embodied in critical reviews and certain other noncommercial uses permitted by copyright law.

For permission requests, write to the author at Irvin@lifeandliesofdumbledore.com

Cover Design: Irvin Khaytman, Copyright ©2018
Portrait of Dumbledore (cover) by Sheila Simmons.
Photo of author by G. M. Courtemanche.

Ordering Information:
Quantity sales. Special discounts are available on quantity purchases by corporations, associations, and others. For details, contact the publisher at orders@lifeandliesofdumbledore.com.

The Life and Lies of Albus Percival Wulfric Brian Dumbledore/ Khaytman, Irvin.—2nd ed.
ISBN: 978-1-7335141-0-1
Library of Congress Control Number: : 2019900922

www.lifeandliesofdumbledore.com

CONTENTS

Dedication i
Author's Note iii
Introduction 1
Chapter 1 5
Chapter 2 25
Chapter 3 43
Chapter 4 67
Chapter 5 87
Chapter 6 115
Chapter 7 171
Epilogue: Judging Dumbledore 181
Appendix A: The Timeline 185
Appendix B: Dumbledore's Most Puzzling Lie 189
Appendix C: Dumbledore as Death 191
Bibliography 195
Acknowledgments 207
About the Author 211

Dedicated to the memory of my dad, who nurtured the beginnings of my love for writing and for *Harry Potter*.

And to my *Harry Potter* family, The Group That Shall Not Be Named, who have kept that love alive all these years.

Author's Note

The Harry Potter fandom is an extraordinary thing—in its breadth, its longevity, and its boundless ingenuity. This is a book first and foremost for the fandom, by a fan. Consequently, it will use a host of jargon developed by the fandom over the last twenty years: abbreviations, portmanteaus, and clever nicknames. While most of them are hopefully self-evident, below is a list of abbreviations frequently used in this book.

There was also a choice to be made about what to call the author of Harry Potter throughout the text. Joanne Rowling has had a closer relationship with her readers than most authors who came before her, and her readers engaged with the material more than most readers had before. One of the things the fandom had to decide relatively early on was what to call her given how often we referred to her—"Rowling," "JKR," or something else.

The question was resolved when she launched her official website in mid-May 2004 and signed the welcome message "With love from J.K. Rowling (Jo to you)."[1] The fansite MuggleNet immediately adopted the convention of calling her "Jo," "because she said to."[2] The entire HP fandom followed suit, and the convention has stuck ever since. I am going to stick

---

[1] https://web.archive.org/web/20040612201127/http://www.jkrowling.com:80/textonly/welcome.cfm
[2] https://web.archive.org/web/20041109105811/http://www.mugglenet.com:80/fusion3/archive.php?show=month&month=May&year=2004

with that convention in this book—who am I to argue with the author's chosen name?

Not to mention, it feels pretty good to be on first-name terms with someone like Jo!

Fandom Terminology

Books
- *Harry Potter and the Sorcerer's Stone*: Book 1, Book One, SS, 1991-1992, first year
- *Harry Potter and the Chamber of Secrets*: Book 2, Book Two, CS, CoS, 1992-1993, second year
- *Harry Potter and the Prisoner of Azkaban*: Book 3, Book Three, PA, PoA, 1993-1994, third year
- *Harry Potter and the Goblet of Fire*: Book 4, Book Four, GF, GoF, 1994-1995, fourth year
- *Harry Potter and the Order of the Phoenix*: Book 5, Book Five, OP, OotP, 1995-1996, fifth year
- *Harry Potter and the Half-Blood Prince*: Book 6, Book Six, HBP, 1996-1997, sixth year
- *Harry Potter and the Deathly Hallows*: Book 7, Book Seven, DH, 1997-1998, seventh year
- *The Tales of Beedle the Bard*: TBB
- *Fantastic Beasts and Where to Find Them*: FB
- *Quidditch through the Ages*: QA

The Battles
- Battle of the Department of Mysteries—climax of *Order of the Phoenix*
- Battle of the Tower—climax of *Half-Blood Prince*
- Battle of the Seven Potters—the aerial battle to get Harry out of Privet Drive in *Deathly Hallows*
- Battle of Hogwarts—the final battle in *Deathly Hallows*

The stages of Voldemort. (Please note that "Voldemort" will often be used interchangeably with most of them, unless the context matters.)
- Tom Riddle—when he's young, up until the murder of Hepzibah Smith, give or take
- Vapormort—when he's "less than the meanest ghost" after the rebounding Avada Kedavra destroys his body
- Quirrellmort—when he's possessing Quirrell
- Babymort—when he has a "rudimentary body" in *Goblet of Fire*
- Voldy—when discussing Peeves's musical stylings, or when he feels cuddly

The Horcruxes, in order of creation
- Diarycrux—Tom Riddle's diary, destroyed by Harry in CoS
- Locketcrux—Slytherin's locket, destroyed by Ron in DH after a very convoluted history
- Ringcrux—Peverell ring (a.k.a. Resurrection Stone), destroyed by Dumbledore between OotP and HBP
- Cupcrux—Hufflepuff's cup, destroyed by Hermione in DH
- Diademcrux—Ravenclaw's diadem, destroyed by Crabbe's Fiendfyre in DH
- Scarcrux—Harry's lightning-bolt scar, destroyed by Voldemort's Killing Curse in DH
- Nagini—Voldemort's pet snake, destroyed by Neville in DH

Referring to events by chapter title
- "The Prince's Tale" (DH)—the twenty memories of Snape's that Harry views in the Pensieve

- "Snape's Worst Memory" (OP)—the memory of Snape's that Harry views in the Pensieve after an Occlumency lesson, when a teenage Snape called Lily a "Mudblood"
- "King's Cross" (DH)—Harry's discussion with Dumbledore in DH after he's been hit with a Killing Curse
- "The Egg and the Eye" (GF)—the congregation of Snape, Filch, Mrs. Norris, Crouch Jr. masquerading as Moody, and Harry under the Invisibility Cloak after Harry goes bathing with his Triwizard egg
- "Padfoot Returns" (GF)—the Trio's meeting with Sirius in Hogsmeade after the Second Task, where they discuss all the mysterious goings-on surrounding the Triwizard Tournament
- "The Madness of Mr. Crouch" (GF)—when a crazy Mr. Crouch shows up at Hogwarts, presents himself to Harry and Viktor Krum, asks for Dumbledore, and then mysteriously disappears (murdered by his son)

Online Resources

The following are the Harry Potter websites frequently mentioned in the text as sources for quotes or ideas; below is some context for each.

Jkrowling.com—Jo's official website from 2004 to 2012, where she would leave puzzles for fans to solve, answer FAQs, dispel rumors, and reveal things like book titles. This was one of the best sources for apocrypha, given that the information came as the books were still being written, and Jo was very meticulous about what she wrote.

MuggleNet.com—Founded in 1999 by Emerson Spartz, MuggleNet was one of the leading HP fansites for the entirety of the Potter fandom. It was most renowned for its editorials, which even Jo mentioned when giving them their fansite award: "... wonderful editorials (more insight there than in several companion volumes I shall not name)." Some of the more frequent contributors to the editorial section became regular columnists.

The Leaky Cauldron (the-leaky-cauldron.org, aka Leaky)—The other big fansite of Potter's heyday, Leaky, was launched in 2000. In 2006, Leaky launched their own essay initiative called Scribbulus, which had monthly "issues" of a handful of essays, often focusing on a particular topic or prompt.

The Harry Potter Lexicon (hp-lexicon.org)—The Lexicon is the supreme online reference tool for Potter canon. Founded in 2000 by Steve Vander Ark, the Lexicon was especially lauded for its painstakingly researched timeline (which was coopted by WB for one of the DVDs). There was also an essay section, which aged well because it was more concerned with parsing the details of the books than with predicting future books.

The Harry Potter Companion (hp-companion.com/)—The HP Companion was launched by a former Lexicon editor, Josie Kearns, in 2009. It is first and foremost a fanart website, presenting fanart for each chapter in the Harry Potter books. However, after all the fanart, Josie Kearns would provide some commentary about each chapter, which spurred very active fan discussions. There's also a small essay section, all written by Josie Kearns, notable for coming after *Deathly Hallows* when most book discussion had quieted.

Should you wish to follow any of the online links provided in the text, they are all provided for your convenience on this book's official website, LifeAndLiesOfDumbledore.com.

Introduction

"There have been about a hundred books written on what Dumbledore knew, how he knew it or why he did what he did."

—*Harry Potter and the Cursed Child*, page 263

We in the Muggle world are not privy to all those books, so this is my attempt to write one. There are many incredible characters in the *Harry Potter* series, but none has fascinated me as much over the years as Albus Percival Wulfric Brian Dumbledore. He is, in many ways, a contradiction: the greatest champion of love, yet a ruthless Machiavellian; seemingly omniscient, yet often making mistakes.

Much like Harry, I revered Dumbledore as the embodiment of all that is good for a solid six and a half books. Then, it turned out Dumbledore was using Harry, "raising him like a pig for slaughter." (DH687) I reread the series half a dozen times after *Deathly Hallows* came out, and I could never reconcile the two. Every time, I would be suckered into loving Dumbledore and would cry at his death; every time, I felt the sting of betrayal in The Prince's Tale and grew furious with him. Once the reread was done, I faced a conundrum: do I view Dumbledore as a saint-like father figure or as cold-hearted and calculating?

To make sense of it all, I embarked upon a mission to unravel just what Dumbledore was up to in the last year of his life: what his plans were and where they went awry. It was quite the undertaking, but it allowed me to make my peace with Dumbledore. As a columnist for the fansite MuggleNet, it was not long before I turned to the earlier books and started the same exercise with each. *Sorcerer's Stone. Prisoner of Azkaban.* Every book I turned to, every part of the story, had Dumbledore pulling the strings behind the scenes. Every odd coincidence and puzzling decision could be explained logically.

I kept writing essays. I started giving presentations at fan conventions. Now, it is time to bring it all together into one coherent narrative. I did my best to follow events chronologically, bringing all my essays together to provide the full story of what Dumbledore was up to during Harry's seven years at Hogwarts. I will present what Dumbledore was doing throughout those years, and only at the end (once we have a better understanding of his actions), will I tackle his character.

I do not claim this to be the definitive story of Dumbledore. Because it's all happening behind the scenes—precisely what makes it all so fascinating—there is a lot of conjecture involved. Assumptions are made, leaps are required, and what I consider the only logical conclusion you may consider poppycock. The astute reader is encouraged to read this book and challenge every bit of it. Every single time I've presented about Dumbledore, a panel attendee has made a brilliant point that opened my eyes to something new.

I am by no means the first to analyze Dumbledore's machinations—I owe a debt of gratitude to many exceedingly clever Harry Potter fans. While I cannot recall every essay I've read on MuggleNet and other websites since 2003, I will highlight some of the most interesting ones in the bibliography. However, I owe a huge debt of gratitude to two writers in particular who have continued to analyze Dumbledore after *Deathly Hallows* was released. I very often disagree with their conclusions, but I love examining their reasoning and engaging in the debate. They will be referenced directly in the text, because I've no wish to claim credit for others' ideas.

First, thanks to mirrormere, whose 2011 essay, "The Flaw in the Plan," first fired in me the desire to analyze Dumbledore's actions.

The biggest debt of all, though, is owed to Josie Kearns, whose essays at the HP Companion, which analyzed the behind-the-scenes of the HP books, were always thought-provoking and often unassailable—on some issues, I disagree with her; on others I just provide concurring opinions and flesh them out.

A note on sources: this book concerns itself with the seven *Harry Potter* novels (page references are to US paperbacks). I will often take J.K. Rowling's words in interviews and her websites to clarify parts of the books that would be murky otherwise. But this book won't engage with other sources of potential canon (whether you acknowledge them as such or not): Pottermore, *Cursed Child, Fantastic Beasts,* etc., do not apply.

So, to Dumbledore.

The series opens with him calling the shots right away in a manner very indicative of how the whole series operates. Hours after an incident occurs (the murder of Lily and James Potter), Dumbledore has a plan in motion to respond. This plan utilizes some arcane magic with which almost no other wizard is familiar: the bond of familial love between the Evans sisters, however strained that relationship was.

And right away, we see Dumbledore covering it up in half-truths: he tells McGonagall that Harry is going to the Dursleys purely to escape his own celebrity. We will come to see this as classic Dumbledore: plausible, even somewhat true, but nowhere near the whole truth. In fact, less charitable readers might call Dumbledore a hypocrite on the subject of honesty. He tells his students, "It is my belief, however, that the truth is generally preferable to lies." (GF722)

Further setting the pattern for the series, McGonagall defers to Dumbledore almost without question. Dumbledore has absolute loyalty from most people on the side of good and is not afraid to use it.

Harry is left with the Dursleys, and Dumbledore has a decade of respite, locking up Death Eaters, rebuilding the wizarding world, and generally not focusing too much on Harry or Voldemort. But in the back of his mind, he knows that eventually the two will have to face off. He keeps tabs on both and perhaps starts brainstorming. But Dumbledore does not have all the information here.

This is a very important point: what Dumbledore knows and when he knows it is as important to figure out as what he was planning and how it went wrong. Many fans operate under the assumption, created by Harry in *Sorcerer's Stone*, that Dumbledore is magically omniscient. He is nothing of the sort—he just has a lot of knowledge and an incredibly impressive analytical mind. We will see both at work throughout this book.

So he can relax through the '80s. But when 1991 rolls around, both Harry and Voldemort reenter the picture. And that is the last moment of peace Dumbledore will ever have. He loses no time in setting a plan in motion before Harry is even retrieved from the Dursleys and is kept busy trying to stay a few steps ahead of Voldemort for the rest of his life.

Chapter 1:
Albus Dumbledore and the Sorcerer's Stone

At the end of *Sorcerer's Stone*, there is a brief exchange among the Trio that first introduces us to the idea of Dumbledore's omniscience:

> "D'you think [Dumbledore] meant you to do it?" said Ron. "Sending you your father's cloak and everything?"
>
> "Well," Hermione exploded, "if he did—I mean to say—that's terrible—you could have been killed."
>
> "No it isn't," said Harry thoughtfully. "He's a funny man, Dumbledore. I think he sort of wanted to give me a chance. I think he knows more or less everything that goes on here, you know. I reckon he had a pretty good idea we were going to try, and instead of stopping us, he just taught us enough to help. I don't think it was an accident he let me find out how the mirror worked. It's almost like he thought I had the right to face Voldemort if I could. . . ." (SS302)

The initial instinct is to just take this at face value—Dumbledore knew everything and planned everything—and just leave it at that... but where would be the fun? Even back in *Sorcerer's Stone*,

Rowling was meticulous enough that it's possible to see Dumbledore's hand moving the chess pieces.

It took me fourteen rereads to figure it all out, and it's very reassuring, because the plot of *Sorcerer's Stone* is among the most nitpicked of the series. More than the other books, a lot of things seem to happen "because... Plot" or "because it's a children's fantasy novel." And while those are valid explanations on occasion, we should generally give Jo more credit than that. There are very few convenient coincidences that can't be explained by Dumbledore at work.

We will tackle the first book from two separate angles. First, we will look at the protections surrounding the Sorcerer's Stone and see what we can glean of Dumbledore's intentions from these protections. Once we know what he hoped to accomplish, we will look at all the events of *Sorcerer's Stone* to see where it's possible to detect Dumbledore's hand pulling the strings.

Protecting the Stone

Let's recap what the protections are:

1. Hagrid provided Fluffy, a gigantic three-headed dog, who could only be gotten past by playing music; a fact that "[n]ot a soul knows except [Hagrid] and Dumbledore" (SS232).
2. Sprout provided Devil's Snare, which Professor Sprout explained in class "likes the dark and the damp" (SS278) and can therefore be fought off by fire. "Conjuring up portable, waterproof fires was a specialty of Hermione's." (CS183)
3. Flitwick charmed a bunch of flying keys, only one of which would open the door; Harry "had a knack for spotting things other people didn't" as "the youngest Seeker in a century." (SS280)

4. McGonagall transfigured a giant chess set to life, on which one had to win a potentially lethal match; wizard chess is Ron's specialty.
5. Quirrell provided a very large troll; Quirrell knocked it out so Harry and Hermione didn't have to, but the Trio had already defeated a troll seven months prior.
6. Snape provided a logic puzzle; the brainy Hermione starts "smiling" when she comes across a logic puzzle she doesn't hesitate to solve (SS285).
7. Dumbledore himself hid the Stone within the Mirror of Erised so "only one who wanted to find the Stone—find it, but not use it—would be able to get it" (SS300).

It's clear to any careful reader that protections two through six are meant to be gotten through specifically by the Trio. Four of the tasks play directly to the Trio's areas of expertise—Seeking, chess, fire, and logic. The other one, the troll, is simply a repeat of what the Trio has already faced. Clearly, Dumbledore meant for Harry and Quirrell to get to the Mirror of Erised. The protections are even designed to be surpassed more than once—hence the potions refill themselves and the chessmen reset themselves. They are also designed for a group of people—hence there are several brooms by the flying keys instead of just one.

Was the wooden flute that Hagrid gifts Harry for Christmas also part of Dumbledore's design? Doubtful, because it's not necessary for getting past Fluffy – it's just a convenience because Harry "didn't feel much like singing." (SS271) The flute we can chalk up to coincidence.

A common point I've seen made is that, far from saving the Stone, Harry actually endangered it. Quirrell could have stared into the Mirror of Erised until he turned blue, and he still would not have the Stone. But then Harry shows up, and the Stone ends up in his pocket, ripe for the taking by Quirrellmort. So if Dumbledore intended for Harry to go after Quirrellmort, why did he also endanger the Stone?

The answer is so simple, it was mostly overlooked until Josie Kearns made the connection. Dumbledore intended Harry and Quirrellmort to face off but for the Stone to remain safely inside the Mirror the entire time.[3]

Dumbledore himself says, "Harry, have you any idea how few wizards could have seen what you saw in that mirror?" (HBP511) Dumbledore could not have known how pure of heart Harry was, how ridiculously selfless he was at the age of eleven. Moreover, Dumbledore had proof to the contrary! A scant five months earlier, Dumbledore watched Harry look into the Mirror of Erised at least twice and knows that Harry sees himself standing with his family. Surely, anyone reasonable would think that this poor boy's deepest desire for the next five months will continue to be to see his family and will not suddenly change to being Voldemort's undoing.

---

[3] In her essay, "Philosopher's Stone - Dumbledore's Perspective," http://hpcompanion.com/ps/psessay/, Josie Kearns ventured the point that Dumbledore meant Harry and Quirrell to face off but didn't expect Harry to get the Stone. I initially disagreed, but upon rereading *Sorcerer's Stone*, I concluded that Josie's hypothesis made the most sense and was therefore correct. The essay is well worth a read; it covers some of the same ground as this one and inspired much of this chapter. I concur with much of it, but Josie attributes more logical leaps to both Dumbledore and Voldemort than I do (a sort of "I did this so you'd know I know you know about that" affair).

As an aside, it's worth wondering how Dumbledore came up with the idea to hide the Stone from any who would covet it for selfish means. He claims, "It was one of my more brilliant ideas." (SS300) To be sure, Dumbledore has plenty of brilliant ideas, but his design for the Stone is awfully close to what he himself did for the Elder Wand.

Dumbledore explains, "I was fit to own the Elder Wand, and not to boast of it, and not to kill with it. I was permitted to tame and to use it, because I took it, not for gain, but to save others from it." (DH720)

Dumbledore had tamed the wand half a century prior because he knew that it was "dangerous, and a lure for fools" (DH713). So Dumbledore knew what to do when presented with another dangerous magical object that was a lure for fools[4]: like the Elder Wand, only one who "took it, not for gain but to save others" (DH720) would be able to get it. Even the language Dumbledore uses is similar: "only one who wanted to find the Stone—find it, but not use it—would be able to get it." (SS300)

Inspired by what he'd learned of the Elder Wand, Dumbledore hides the Stone in the Mirror of Erised, convinced that neither Quirrell nor Harry will get it out. Dumbledore intends for Harry to face off against Quirrellmort without endangering the Stone. But like most of Dumbledore's best-laid plans, this goes terribly awry when Harry looks into the Mirror and gets the Stone, and suddenly Quirrellmort's attention is focused on Harry instead of the Mirror.

---

[4] "As much money and life as you could want! The two things most human beings would choose above all—the trouble is, humans do have a knack of choosing precisely those things that are worst for them." (SS297) This is Dumbledore's much gentler way of calling the Stone a lure for fools—after all, he's speaking to an eleven-year-old.

Why does Dumbledore orchestrate all of this? Because Harry needs the experience facing off against Voldemort. Dumbledore explains, "I knew not whether it would be ten, twenty or fifty years before he returned, but I was sure he would do so, and I was sure, too, knowing him as I have done, that he would not rest until he killed [Harry]." (OP835)

Dumbledore knows that the time will come—hopefully much later, but eventually it will come—for Harry to face off against Voldemort. Dumbledore's goal from the minute Harry steps into Hogwarts is to give Harry his best fighting chance—because according to the prophecy, Harry is the wizarding world's best chance to vanquish Voldemort. Dumbledore wants Harry's first attempt at facing off against Voldemort to happen in as controlled an environment as possible. And such an opportunity falls into Dumbledore's lap just as Harry is coming to Hogwarts!

Dumbledore knows that "Quirrell, full of hatred, greed, and ambition, sharing his soul with Voldemort, could not touch [Harry]" because of Lily's sacrifice (SS299). So this would have been as good a trial run as was possible: Harry would face off against Quirrell, he would emerge victorious because Quirrell cannot touch him, and that will be that. The Stone's not in danger; Harry isn't in too much danger. Not only will this give Harry experience, it will also be an important confidence booster to a kid who's been downtrodden most of his life.

In fact, that's the more crucial aspect: going forward, Harry needs the confidence of having faced off against Voldemort. He needs to not lose his head when he comes face to face with Voldemort. Indeed, by the time Voldemort returns to his body, Harry is an old pro at facing him—he's faced Voldemort more often than he's taken exams!

Admittedly, Dumbledore probably wished this whole Voldemort-fighting dress rehearsal would happen later than Harry's first year, but he is quite adept at pivoting and changing plans as necessary. An important bit of perspective to always maintain is that the characters don't know they're in a seven-book series. Dumbledore explains to Harry (again in that invaluable *Order of the Phoenix* confession), "You rose magnificently to the challenge that faced you, and sooner—much sooner—than I had expected, you found yourself face-to-face with Voldemort." (OP837)

This refers to Dumbledore's expectations before all this Quirrell stuff went down. When Dumbledore got wind of what was going on, he moved up his timeline and set up the showdown for Harry's first year.

This same reasoning explains the presence of protections two through six. At first glance, why bother with all the "protections" surrounding the Stone? Only two of them were even remotely effective: Fluffy and the Mirror of Erised. The rest of them—Sprout's Devil's Snare, Flitwick's flying keys, McGonagall's chess board, and Snape's riddle—are gotten through by a trio of first years and don't serve to hinder Quirrell at all.

Dumbledore tells Harry, "I have watched you more closely than you can have imagined." (OP839) But along with watching Harry, he watched Ron and Hermione, once it became evident that they would be Harry's closest friends and staunchest allies.

It's made clear in the latter books that Dumbledore has been watching Harry's friends. He tells Harry in *Half-Blood Prince*, "I think you ought to relax [the decision to tell no one about the prophecy] in favor of your friends, Mr. Ronald Weasley and Miss Hermione Granger." (HBP78) He also gives Harry permission to tell Ron and Hermione about his forays into Voldemort's past via Pensieve, saying, "I think Mr. Weasley and Miss Granger have proved themselves trustworthy." (HBP215)

It's easy to dismiss this, but Dumbledore is perhaps the least trusting character in the series. He gives his closest allies the absolute bare minimum of information necessary and does not wholly confide in anyone. Yet he instructs Harry to reveal to Ron and Hermione things that are known only to Harry and Dumbledore himself. This is a big deal. Dumbledore would not place such trust lightly, so this is evidence that he knows a great deal about Harry's friends.

We also see this come into play when he leaves both of them items in his will, despite making "exceptionally few personal bequests." (DH124) He gave Ron the Deluminator, knowing that Ron's commitment to the Horcrux hunt might waver (DH391). He gave Hermione *The Tales of Beedle the Bard* to decipher and trusted her to combat Harry's rash nature (DH720).[5]

But back in *Sorcerer's Stone*, Dumbledore did not yet know if Ron and Hermione would be the staunch allies that Harry would later need. He needed a way to cement their collaboration for the future. And what better way than to have them help Harry get to Quirrell? So he decided to put in some barriers specifically for the trio to work their way through. This gives them valuable experience working together through magical obstacles as well as confidence in having triumphed. And this is the reason for protections two through six, tailored specifically to their strengths—to establish the Trio as we know it.

An interesting theory I've come across, lately in Lorrie Kim's *SNAPE: A Definitive Reading* (p. 18), is that Dumbledore's original intention was for Neville to also be part of the crew that went through the trapdoor. Ergo, the Devil's Snare was an obstacle meant for him, given his strength in Herbology. It's a good theory but

---

[5] Dumbledore's bequest to Hermione will factor into the sixth chapter, Albus Dumbledore and the Half-Blood Prince.

does not really gel with how meticulous Dumbledore is about these things.

Neville's proficiency at Herbology is not as overt in *Sorcerer's Stone*; the first time it's mentioned is Neville getting a "good Herbology mark making up for his abysmal Potions one," (SS307) in the closing pages of the book. Hermione's aptitude for fires seems to be more indicative of facing off against Devil's Snare.

More importantly, if Dumbledore watched Harry's friendships as closely as we believe, he would have known Neville would not be included. The only times Neville is together with the Trio is watching Quidditch matches, during the late-night Norbert fiasco, and in the ensuing detention. Not exactly bosom friends, and Neville's being misinformed about Norbert further indicates lack of confidence. The Devil's Snare is the first obstacle after Fluffy; Dumbledore could have gone at any point and removed it once he figured out Neville wouldn't be part of the quest.

Dumbledore is meticulous about the setup here. All the tasks are designed to be passed through by the whole trio... until the last one before the Mirror, Snape's potion puzzle. Here, there is a potion to move backwards as well as forwards—what is the need of this, if not to send Ron and Hermione back to safety? And as for the potion to move on to the next room: "There's only enough for one of us" (SS286). Yet there's no mention of there being not enough potion for more than one person to go back. The intention is clear: only Harry is to move on and face Quirrell, while Hermione and Ron are to go back.

Why is this? Because Ron and Hermione, unlike Harry, have no magical protection from Quirrellmort. And Dumbledore does care about students' safety, to some extent. So he doesn't want to send Ron and Hermione into the fray, knowing they'll likely be hurt—especially given Voldemort's propensity for taking hostages. Oh yes, Dumbledore planned every detail very carefully indeed.

So, the next question to answer is why Dumbledore had Quirrell provide one of the protections if he so clearly suspected Quirrell by that point? Not only does this make Quirrell's job that much easier—by allowing him to know what the other protections are—but this could also hinder the trio. Sure, they took out a troll before, but as McGonagall says in the first movie, it was "sheer dumb luck."

I believe that Dumbledore did this with the intention of protecting Ron and Hermione—he needed Quirrell to get to the Mirror without issue so only Harry would face him. If Quirrell hadn't been privy to the protections surrounding the Stone, he might have actually been stumped by them—maybe he's terrible at chess! (Side note: I now have a great mental image of Quirrell playing countless chess matches against Voldemort as practice for this one.)

If Quirrell couldn't get past the chess board or any other obstacle, he would have run into the entire Trio there. And he likely would not have hesitated to kill them. To reiterate, Ron and Hermione have no protection from him, and Dumbledore would have wanted to prevent them facing off against Quirrell. Hence, Dumbledore includes Quirrell in "protecting" the Stone in order to make Quirrell's job easier and make sure he's well ahead of the Trio.

It's also worth noting that Dumbledore probably supervised these protections extremely closely. He likely did not tell the professors his reasons, but I could believe he suggested the individual protections to each professor and made a sufficiently convincing case that they listened. He probably ensured that Professor Sprout would mention Devil's Snare in class, since that plant seems to be rather different from the usual curriculum in Herbology (the younger students don't generally deal with deadly plants).

The exception to this might be Snape's puzzle—that one seems to fit Dumbledore's plans so exactly that it's hard to believe it wasn't micromanaged. Perhaps Dumbledore trusted Snape enough to reveal the plan. But I think it's more likely Dumbledore just told Snape exactly what had to be done without explaining himself, and Snape obeyed because he knew to trust Dumbledore despite his secretive ways.

Dumbledore's Invisible Hand

Now that we know Dumbledore's end goal—to have Harry face off against Quirrell to gain some valuable experience—let's examine how he imperceptibly influenced events for an entire year to get there.

Dumbledore has sources that keep him informed of Voldemort's doings; in Book 2 they let Dumbledore know that Voldemort "is currently in hiding in the forests of Albania." (CS328) So when these sources inform him that Voldemort is gone from Albania in 1991, Dumbledore knows to fear for the Sorcerer's Stone.

He also knows that Quirrell was recently there, so Dumbledore probably suspects him to some degree. But Dumbledore is not sure and wants to find out what's up. He decides he wants the race for the Stone to happen at Hogwarts, where he can keep an eye on things. It's probably at this time that he concocts his plan to have Harry face off against Voldemort, so he has Hagrid pick up the Stone from Gringotts, in full view of Harry, giving Harry the first clue.

There is really no other reason why Hagrid was picking up the Stone as part of his and Harry's trip to Diagon Alley, considering wizards can just Apparate to Diagon Alley whenever they need to. Admittedly, the one bit that cannot be easily explained away is Quirrell attempting his Gringotts robbery hours after Hagrid retrieves the Stone. I suppose one could come up with a convoluted explanation of how Dumbledore dictated the timing of this event, but I am comfortable calling this one a coincidence and moving on. I set very little store in coincidences in Rowling's world, but they do happen, and on those rare occasions I'll accept them as such.

Then, as soon as the school year starts, Dumbledore proceeds to set Quirrell (if Quirrell is indeed Voldemort's agent) on the trail of the Stone. At the Start-of-Term Feast, Dumbledore makes a very public announcement that "the third-floor corridor on the right-hand side is out of bounds to everyone who does not wish to die a very painful death." (SS127)

Honestly, he might as well have whispered in Quirrell's ear, "Psssst! That's where I'm hiding the Stone!" Even Percy notes how strange this announcement is, "because he usually gives us a reason why we're not allowed to go somewhere." (SS127) But Quirrell takes the bait—hook, line, and sinker. The very next morning, Harry and Ron are rescued on the third-floor corridor "by Professor Quirrell, who was passing." (SS132)

Dumbledore notices this, and tells Snape, "Keep an eye on Quirrell, won't you?" (DH679) We don't know precisely when this "Prince's Tale" flashback takes place, but since Snape is ranting and raving about Harry, we can assume it was around the second or third week of the term. Dumbledore's plan is working beautifully, since a week into the school year, he has already confirmed that Quirrell is the one after the Stone.

Meanwhile, Dumbledore drops another hint to Harry in the form of the news article about the Gringott's break-in that Harry finds at Hagrid's. Isn't it odd that Hagrid would have a five-week-old news clipping lying around? I'm betting Dumbledore put it there for Harry to find—clearly, Dumbledore is using Hagrid to unwittingly feed Harry information.

Hagrid has also provided the first line of defense for the Stone. Fluffy has a very specific role to play—otherwise, as Ron says, "What do they think they're doing, keeping a thing like that locked up in a school?" (SS161) The Stone was perfectly safe within the Mirror, so why have a murderous three-headed dog sitting in the school, behind a door that's susceptible to a basic Alohomora charm?

This is the first time we see that Dumbledore very much likes to control when things happen to suit his purpose, and that's where Fluffy comes in. Keep that tendency in mind, as it will be an absolutely crucial concept when we get to *Deathly Hallows*. Fluffy is there to slow everything down, to allow Dumbledore to set the stage for Harry to go after Quirrell. He wants Harry to learn some magic, and he also wants to learn more about the boy before sending him to face Voldemort. If Quirrell got right to the Mirror, he would take it and scamper, and there goes Dumbledore's plan for the Harry vs. Voldemort showdown. But trying to figure out how to get past Fluffy would keep Quirrell busy for quite some time.

Keep in mind that at this point, none of the other protections are in place. We only learn of protections other than Fluffy in February, when the Trio assumes there must be other things guarding the Stone (SS227), and it's not confirmed by Hagrid until weeks later (SS232), which is in April, according to the HP Lexicon's timeline.[6]

The fact that the protections are tailored to the Trio means that they had to be put in place once

---

[6] https://legacy.hp-lexicon.org/timelines/calendars/calendar_ps.html In general, I will use the Lexicon's timelines to refer to when things happened; they are an invaluable resource for HP fans.

Dumbledore actually knew who Harry's closest friends would be. Therefore, the very earliest the protections could have been constructed is November, since Hermione wasn't even friendly with Harry until Halloween.[7] Allow a few weeks to learn that Hermione really had become Harry's friend for good and for Dumbledore to learn more about Hermione, and it seems unlikely the protections were put in place earlier than December. But I think it may have been later than that.

We know that between September and December, Fluffy was in place, and protections two through six were not. But was the Mirror, with the Stone in it, in place at this time? No.

Dumbledore would not have wanted to risk Quirrell getting past Fluffy and fleeing with the Mirror before Harry had a chance to face him. Dumbledore, while making fanfare about Fluffy and what it's guarding, actually kept the Mirror and the Stone elsewhere. It doesn't matter where, since no one would know that the Stone was hidden inside the Mirror... for all we know, maybe it was in Dumbledore's office the whole time! And meanwhile, he let Quirrell get on with trying to get past Fluffy, perhaps chortling at the thought of how peeved Voldemort would be if they did get past Fluffy and found nothing there.

Either way, after four months of this, it's the Christmas holidays—Quirrell still hasn't figured out

---

[7] While not canonical, there is further evidence in *Journey Through a History of Magic* (p. 30), where we become privy to Jo's drafts of certain passages in the books. In one such draft, Quirrell states in no uncertain terms that he was trying to "see what was guarding the Stone" aside from Fluffy, meaning he (and the other professors) have not yet put their obstacles in place. Even though this was only in a draft, it shows that Jo's original intention was to not have the obstacles present until after Halloween.

how to get past Fluffy, and Dumbledore believes he knows enough about the Trio to start setting up the obstacles. But before that can happen, Harry needs to be told about the Mirror of Erised—having his first encounter with the Mirror happen during his faceoff with Quirrell could be disastrous! (Picture Voldemort convincing the naïve eleven-year-old that what he sees in the Mirror will come to pass if Voldemort is resurrected). As Dumbledore tells Harry, "If you ever do run across it, you will now be prepared." (SS214) So Dumbledore takes the Mirror out of hiding, wherever it was, to show to Harry.[8]

I don't think there's any doubt that Dumbledore followed Harry on Christmas night. That was the day Harry got his Invisibility Cloak, and Dumbledore would have known that Harry would take it for a spin—the timing of Dumbledore giving it to him, like everything else, was deliberate. Let's face it, the odds of Harry stumbling onto the one room with the Mirror are astronomical. Counting on Harry's adventurous nature, Dumbledore probably waited outside the Gryffindor common room for Harry to emerge, followed him invisibly, and put the Mirror into the room that Harry was about to enter. Then, he likely watched with tears in his eyes as Harry looked into the Mirror and saw his

---

[8] The Red Hen has an intriguing alternative for why Dumbledore chose to show Harry the Mirror of Erised: it was a test of Harry's character to ensure that he was not like Tom Riddle. I disagree for two reasons. First, Dumbledore has been observing Harry very closely for four months and should have the measure of his character by now. Second, Dumbledore does not have any alternatives who have "the power to vanquish the Dark Lord"—there's no point testing if Harry is good enough because he *has* to be good enough. http://www.redhen-publications.com/quirrelldebacle.html

family—the same vision that Dumbledore himself sees.⁹

Dumbledore may have hoped that Harry would figure out what the Mirror did on his own, but Harry doesn't, not even when he brings Ron the following night. And Dumbledore sees that Harry is consumed by what the Mirror shows him, so on the third night he finally shows himself to Harry and explains what the Mirror does. Then he says, "The Mirror will be moved to a new home tomorrow." (SS213) Note that it's a "new" home—I believe that this is when the Mirror was put underneath Fluffy's trapdoor for the first time. And after the Mirror was in place, Dumbledore had McGonagall, Flitwick, Sprout, Snape, and Quirrell put their protections in place in early January.

Things then quiet down for a while, until Quirrell gets Hagrid drunk and finds out how to get past Fluffy. Meanwhile, unbeknownst to Dumbledore, the Trio has been sleuthing and made the Nicolas Flamel connection, realizing that the Sorcerer's Stone is what Fluffy is guarding. We know that Dumbledore is unaware of this because he is surprised by Harry's knowledge of Flamel (SS297).

After Quirrell finds out about Fluffy, his behavior likely tips Dumbledore off, and Dumbledore now needs to let the Trio know about the Stone. But Dumbledore doesn't want his involvement to be known, so he waits for an opportunity to let Harry know in an inconspicuous way. And just such an opportunity

---

[9] Bloomsbury Live Chat with J.K. Rowling; July 30th, 2007, http://www.accio-quote.org/articles/2007/0730-bloomsbury-chat.html,
Allie: *What did dumbledore truly see in the mirror of erised*
J.K. Rowling: He saw his family alive, whole and happy – Ariana, Percival and Kendra all returned to him, and Aberforth reconciled to him."

presents itself when Harry and Hermione land themselves in detention!

At this point, something has been killing the unicorns in the Forbidden Forest, and Dumbledore has likely put two and two together and realized it's Voldemort. Dumbledore sees this as a good opportunity to tip Harry off about the Stone and about the fact that Voldemort is after it. He decides that the detention will take place in the Forbidden Forest.

This is the only plausible explanation for that detention. Even by Hogwarts's very lax standards, sending four first years into the Forest at night, when they realistically are no help in finding a dead unicorn, is absurd. It's certainly not McGonagall's style, and until Dolores Umbridge comes along, the detentions mostly consist of cleaning and other sensible things. The idea for this detention was almost certainly part of Dumbledore's plan.

One thing that always struck me as odd was that Firenze knew about the Stone. He is the one who helps lead Harry to the conclusion that Voldemort is trying to steal the Sorcerer's Stone—after explaining what unicorn blood does, he asks Harry, "Mr. Potter, do you know what is hidden in the school at this very moment?" (SS259) Why would Firenze, a centaur who has nothing to do with anything, know about it? Unless the meaning of "Mars is bright tonight" is "There's a Sorcerer's Stone hidden at Hogwarts," there's no way for Firenze to know about it... unless Dumbledore tipped him off. After Dumbledore planned Harry's excursion into the Forest, he likely sought out the most approachable centaur and instructed Firenze to watch over Harry and tell him about the Stone and Voldemort at an opportune moment.[10]

Did Dumbledore plan the meeting in the forest between Harry and Quirrell? I'm leaning towards no, because that would needlessly endanger Harry and the other students. Also, Dumbledore doesn't really have a way of knowing which nights Quirrell goes to drink the unicorn blood. I think we can give Quirrell enough benefit of the doubt to not drink it on a regular schedule. That run-in was a coincidence, but luckily Firenze was watching over Harry, and no harm was done.

Another subtle clue of Dumbledore's involvement is that he returns the Invisibility Cloak to Harry that night. Why that night, of all of them? Because Dumbledore counted on Harry now knowing what's going on and equipped him with the Cloak to go after Quirrell.

Now the only thing for Dumbledore to do is to leave and allow events to unfold. Perhaps Quirrell just happened to choose the last day of Harry's exams to send Dumbledore away, or perhaps Dumbledore waited until the exams were done so as not to interfere with Harry's education. Either way, about a week after the incursion into the Forest, Dumbledore gets an

---

[10] In *Sorcerer's Stone*, the other centaurs (namely Bane) are upset at the meddling in what happens to Harry in the Forest. Ironically enough, many years later Dumbledore would set things in motion to fulfill what the centaurs saw in the heavens. Harry supposes that "Bane thinks Firenze should have let Voldemort kill me.... I suppose that's written in the stars as well." (SS260) Indeed, that is probably what was written in the stars, as Harry lets Voldemort kill him in that very forest during the Battle of Hogwarts. Bane was just trying to rush things along instead of waiting another six years. (Credit to Eileen Jones at the *Lexicon* for this observation, in her piece "Bane Was Right All Along." https://www.hp-lexicon.org/2018/01/31/bane-right-along/)

urgent owl from the Ministry and "leaves," allowing Quirrell and the Trio to go after the Stone.

Here we get evidence that Dumbledore's staff is not privy to the plan for the Trio to go through the trapdoor. When Harry reveals he knows about the Stone, "Whatever Professor McGonagall had expected, it wasn't that. The books she was carrying tumbled out of her arms, but she didn't pick them up." (SS267) So unless McGonagall is just having a laugh and doing a bit of acting (there is a theory that she carries a stack of books around just so she can keep dropping them for dramatic effect), this means that the staff was not aware that the protections they were creating were custom-made for the Trio. This is very much Dumbledore's style; he will employ a similar lack of disclosure in *Order of the Phoenix*, when he assigns tasks to his allies.

Did Dumbledore actually go to London? Perhaps, but if he did, he certainly got back much sooner than he leads us to believe. Hermione tells Harry, "I brought Ron around—that took a while—and we were dashing up to the owlery to contact Dumbledore when we met him in the entrance hall—he already knew—he just said, 'Harry's gone after him, hasn't he?' and hurtled off to the third floor." (SS302)

Dumbledore is all about timing. He wanted to give Harry some time to face off against Quirrell but would then dash in to end things. So he carefully planned it. After the potions puzzle, Harry would go to fight Quirrell, while Ron and Hermione would return. Dumbledore watched them go, waited for Ron and Hermione to emerge, which would be his cue to go after Harry—that would give Harry enough time.

What Dumbledore hadn't counted on was Ron getting injured and Hermione having to take time to revive him. He was frantic by the time Ron and Hermione got to him: he knew that they should have emerged sooner. That's why Dumbledore "feared [he] might be too late." (SS297) He also must have received quite a shock when he arrived and saw the Sorcerer's Stone was no longer in the mirror! That was his first sign that he was dealing with an extraordinary boy.

Upon reflection, Harry was quite right—Dumbledore did orchestrate much of what happened that year at Hogwarts. All the protections surrounding the Stone were meticulously planned by Dumbledore for the Trio. Some parts of the plan went wrong—like Harry getting the Stone out of the mirror and Ron getting injured. And there were quite a few coincidences—Quirrell trying to steal the Stone just after it was taken, Harry meeting Quirrell in the Forest, and Harry finding out about Nicolas Flamel.

But on the whole, this plan turned out all right. Throughout the year, no one was really the wiser about Dumbledore's scheming, and Harry now has his first victory over Voldemort. To be sure, this all seems like a lot of effort for Dumbledore. But Dumbledore has the luxury of having time to set up such elaborate plots, because the wizarding world is at peace. Now that it's all resolved, Dumbledore can relax... until the next crisis rears its head.

Chapter 2:
Albus Dumbledore and the Chamber of Secrets

After the events of *Sorcerer's Stone*, Dumbledore must have been optimistic that he (and Harry) would have some time to relax. Voldemort just got trounced by an eleven-year-old and is off haunting Albania again. Nothing for Dumbledore to worry about besides Fudge pestering him. He is not even concerned about telling Harry about the prophecy yet: "I was too happy to think that I did not have to do it on that particular day. You were too young, much too young."[11] (OP838)

For the first two months of the school year, Dumbledore does remain relatively worry-free, give or take an incident with a flying car. But his serene existence comes crashing down on Halloween with a Petrified cat and some dramatic graffiti, declaring that "The Chamber of Secrets Has Been Opened."

At this point, Dumbledore knows that Tom Riddle is the last remaining descendant of Salazar Slytherin (CS333) and is fairly confident that Riddle opened the Chamber the last time, fifty years ago. So he knows that Voldemort is somehow behind it, but a quick check of his sources will reveal that Voldemort is still in Albania. So, as he says to McGonagall, "The question is not who. The question is how. . . ." (CS181)

---

[11] For more about Dumbledore's conversation with Harry, see Appendix B.

Foiled by a Malfoy for the First Time

Dumbledore is very rarely at a loss as to what's going on, but he is tripped up (rather hilariously) by Lucius Malfoy's spite. As most fans who have delved into HP theorizing have come to accept, Lucius's original plan was to plant the diary on Harry, which would lead to Harry's expulsion, at the very least. However, Lucius gets so angry at Mr. Weasley at Flourish & Blotts that instead, he impulsively plants the diary on Ginny in an act of pure spite. I won't bother expounding on this theory, as many other writers have already done so.[12]

This is the crucial piece of information that Dumbledore is missing. He watches Harry and his friends very closely but does not extend the same scrutiny to Ginny Weasley. If Lucius had proceeded with the original plan, Dumbledore would have figured it out in a heartbeat, and *Chamber of Secrets* would have been a much shorter book. But the elder Malfoy's impetuosity proved to be the biggest factor in his limited success; Dumbledore can reason his way out of any situation, but he has a harder time dealing with people being irrational.

The irony is that Dumbledore may actually be responsible, in a roundabout way, for the headache Lucius Malfoy causes him that year. Lucius Malfoy does care for his son, and Draco came home from Hogwarts rather upset about how things were going.

When we meet Draco at Borgin & Burkes after Harry has a Floo Powder mishap, he is sullenly complaining about favoritism at Hogwarts (CS50).

---

[12] Josie Kearns writes about this in "What Did Dobby Know?" at the HP Companion, https://hpcompanion.com/essays/csessay/. Steve Connolly also wrote about this, pre-DH, over at MuggleNet, http://www.mugglenet.com/2007/03/dumbledores-master-plan-part-3/.

Lucius's responses to Draco indicate that this topic has come up frequently over the summer. While the initial impression given is that of Draco being a whiner, his grievances are not without merit.

Under the veneer of being far removed from the day-to-day life of Hogwarts,[13] Dumbledore is no less partisan towards his house than Snape or McGonagall. In *Sorcerer's Stone*, for example, McGonagall "speak[s] to Professor Dumbledore [to] see if we can't bend the first-year rule" (SS152) to allow Harry to join the Gryffindor Quidditch Team. Given that Harry winds up on the Quidditch team, Dumbledore must have given the okay. As Hermione puts it, this is "a reward for breaking rules" (SS166) that is horribly unfair to just about the entire student body.[14] Would it really have been so terrible if Harry waited another year before joining the Quidditch team?

But the event that irredeemably ruined Dumbledore's image for all Slytherins was the Leaving Feast in *Sorcerer's Stone*, where Dumbledore goes out of his way to crush the Slytherins' hopes. Dumbledore is perfectly within his rights to award points to the Trio for going on an adventure, and to Neville for

---

[13] It's telling that in *Sorcerer's Stone*, Dumbledore making an appearance at a Quidditch match has all of Hogwarts in a tizzy. There are six Quidditch matches per year, so it doesn't seem like an unreasonable burden for a headmaster to be present at all of them. But Dumbledore makes it clear that he cannot be bothered to watch his students play Quidditch, remaining aloof and distant from the student body.

[14] It is unfair to the other houses, who are not allowed to play any promising first years of their own. It is unfair to the older students in Gryffindor House, many of whom never got the chance to join the team—since the whole team aside from Oliver is third year and under, the entire Quidditch team must have graduated in 1990/1991, leaving students in the Class of 1992 through 1995 out of luck after Harry and Katie Bell joined the team.

standing up to friends. However, the way he does it is unnecessarily cruel to a quarter of the school.

Dumbledore lets the entire school go into the Leaving Feast, thinking Slytherin had won the house cup. The Great Hall

> was decked out in the Slytherin colors of green and silver to celebrate Slytherin's winning the house cup for the seventh year in a row. A huge banner showing the Slytherin serpent covered the wall behind the High Table. (SS304)

Is that enough of a fake-out? No. Dumbledore then lists the points totals, all but announcing that Slytherin had won. "A storm of cheering and stamping broke out from the Slytherin table." Harry isn't happy about it, but one has to imagine that this meant an awful lot to the Slytherins—especially the first years, who'd never won the house cup before, and had spent a year being instilled with the belief that winning the house cup is of paramount importance.

> "Yes, Yes, well done, Slytherin," said Dumbledore. "However, recent events must be taken into account."
>
> The room went very still. The Slytherins' smiles faded a little. (SS305)

Dumbledore has a flair for the theatrical, and he draws this out for maximum effect. He announces the points for the trio, one by one. He makes sure to give just enough points to tie Gryffindor with Slytherin, for maximum drama. There are no guidelines for how many points are awarded for playing chess or for "pure nerve," so this is Dumbledore choosing point totals purely to stage a spectacle for an audience. At that point, the Slytherins are surely thinking, "Fine, even if we tied, at least we still won." And then Dumbledore goes ahead and crushes the Slytherins by awarding Neville ten points.

> "Which means," Dumbledore called over the storm of applause, for even Ravenclaw and Hufflepuff were celebrating the downfall of Slytherin, "we need a little change of decoration."
>
> He clapped his hands. In an instant, the green hangings became scarlet and the silver became gold; the huge Slytherin serpent vanished and a towering Gryffindor lion took its place. (SS306)

It's small wonder that Draco leaves his first year thoroughly disenchanted with his headmaster. He spends all of second year parroting Lucius: "Father's always said old Dumbledore's the worst thing that's ever happened to this place." (CS222)

This is a big change of pace from *Sorcerer's Stone*, where Hagrid refers to Dumbledore as "the greatest headmaster Hogwarts ever had." (SS58)[15] It's made clear later in *Chamber of Secrets* that a lot of Hogwarts students share Hagrid's assessment: when McGonagall tells the Great Hall that she has "good news" at the end of the year, the very first guess is "Dumbledore's

---

[15] This is some of the first evidence that we should approach Hagrid's broad declarative statements with skepticism. Hagrid's worldview is simplistic, as one can tell both here and in the wholly incorrect statement: "there wasn't a witch or wizard who went bad who wasn't in Slytherin." (SS80)

coming back!" several people yelled joyfully. (CS284)[16] But there is an important difference between the reverence for Dumbledore being widespread and being unanimous; it's telling that Draco seems perfectly at home disparaging Dumbledore in front of the Slytherins.

In *The Tales of Beedle the Bard*, Dumbledore refers to his enmity with Lucius Malfoy and attributes it to a disagreement about the appropriateness of the fairytales available in the Hogwarts Library. "This exchange marked the beginning of Mr. Malfoy's long campaign to have me removed from my post as Headmaster of Hogwarts, and of mine to have him removed from his position as Lord Voldemort's Favorite Death Eater." (TBB42)

However, one can't help noticing that this enmity really seemed to foment after Lucius's son came home from his first year at Hogwarts very upset about Dumbledore's disregard for the Slytherins. This may explain why Lucius chose that particular year to put in motion his plan to reopen the Chamber of Secrets, which he must have known would provide him an opportunity to remove Dumbledore from office.

Dumbledore Lacking Information

Dumbledore's reasoning must surely have clued him in as to the identity of Slytherin's monster. Unlike Harry and his friends, Dumbledore is definitely familiar with various fantastic beasts and where to find them. There must be a very small number of creatures that can kill, Petrify, live for a thousand years, and be

---

[16] The notability of this moment was first brought to my attention by Eileen Jones in a *Harry Potter Lexicon Minute*. "What a beacon of hope the Headmaster must be to illicit this kind of reaction," she writes. https://www.hp-lexicon.org/2018/12/19/cs16-ginny-and-dumbledore/

controlled only by descendants of a Parselmouth. Dumbledore either shares his suspicions with Snape, or Snape (being very clever in his own right) comes to the same conclusion independently. Either way, Snape takes matters into his own hands at the fateful Dueling Club meeting.

The spell Snape instructs Draco to use—Serpensortia—makes no sense in a dueling context. As online commenter Irene M. Cesca put it: "You throw a snake at your opponent and... What?! You cross your fingers that you're dueling Indiana Jones and that he's gonna run out screaming like a little kid?"[17] There was something else going on. This is something I've puzzled over quite a bit, occasionally tempted to just go with the "Because Plot" explanation, but I think we can make sense of it.

It's definitely not Dumbledore's doing—Dumbledore likes to run controlled experiments, and throwing a snake into the middle of the student body isn't his style. Snape seems surprised by Harry's Parselmouth abilities, so Snape was not confirming his own theory about Harry. It would appear to me that Snape, knowing the Heir of Slytherin was likely a Parselmouth, was hoping to unmask him or her at the Dueling Club. Humiliating Harry in the process would be a bonus. But Snape is shocked by Harry being the Parselmouth because, whatever else he may think of Harry, it doesn't make sense to him that Harry is the Heir of Slytherin.

Dumbledore is informed of this. The next day, Justin Finch-Fletchley and Nearly Headless Nick are Petrified, and Dumbledore meets with Harry in his

---

[17] Part of the chapter discussion at The Harry Potter Companion, https://hpcompanion.com/cs/cs11/.

office.[18] He tells Hagrid right away, "I do not think that Harry attacked those people." (CS208) But Dumbledore still wants to pick Harry's brain. He performs Legilimency on Harry during that meeting and gets quite a bit of material: Draco Malfoy shouting about Mudbloods, a plot concerning Polyjuice, Harry hearing a disembodied voice, and Harry's fears about his reputation (CS209). So Dumbledore remains as confused as ever.

In the meantime, we see firsthand through some flashbacks where the pattern of Dumbledore's favoritism of Gryffindors over Slytherins began: in the 1940s, with Tom Riddle and Rubeus Hagrid. Tom Riddle pointed the finger of blame at Hagrid for opening the Chamber of Secrets and killing Moaning Myrtle. Hagrid was expelled, but Dumbledore got him to stay on as assistant gamekeeper. Dumbledore was rightfully suspicious of Tom Riddle,[19] and Hagrid was indeed innocent of opening the Chamber of Secrets.

However, there is a larger pattern at work here: when a Gryffindor commits a crime, Dumbledore goes out of his way to ameliorate the sentence and protect the Gryffindor. Hagrid, though not responsible for Myrtle's death, was raising an acromantula inside the school. Maybe this is my arachnophobia talking, but that does not sound like innocence to me. Hagrid was raising an illegal creature that actively eats humans

---

[18] The reader is treated to a rather delightful pun here: the knocker on the door to Dumbledore's office is shaped like a griffin (CS204), making it a *literal* Gryffindo[o]r. I'm inclined to think this was Dumbledore's creation; he certainly seems the type of headmaster to make his office door into a pun.

[19] Tom Riddle charms every member of the faculty except Dumbledore. This is an ironic role reversal of what happens in the books' present day: where usually Snape is railing to Headmaster Dumbledore against his favorite; back then Dumbledore kept trying to convince Headmaster Dippet not to favor Tom Riddle so much.

inside a school. Sure, he trained Aragog well enough to tame his human-eating nature. . . but that doesn't erase the danger nor the illegality of his actions. I'd expel anyone who raised giant spiders in my school. But Hagrid remains at Hogwarts as assistant gamekeeper and keeps an illicit wand in his umbrella.[20] Dumbledore remains loyal to Hagrid, culminating in a very questionable decision to make Hagrid a professor after his name is cleared in 1993. Perhaps if Grubbly-Plank had been a Gryffindor, she would not have been passed over for the job.[21]

Help Will Always Be Given

Back to the present: to Dumbledore's great chagrin, he remains helpless for the rest of the school year. Lucius Malfoy even manages a short-lived triumph in his campaign to remove Dumbledore and ousts Dumbledore from Hogwarts. It's not hard to imagine this as Dumbledore's darkest hour—removed from Harry and Hogwarts with a basilisk on the loose. It's doubtful that Dumbledore ever wanted Harry mixed up in all this—Harry's first year was enough of a trial run, and having him face off against a basilisk could end very badly indeed. But it's out of Dumbledore's hands, and Harry is involved, so Dumbledore helps him as best he can.

---

[20] A pre-DH theory that I found engaging comes courtesy of Maline Freden at MuggleNet (North Tower #27: "Wands and Where to Find Them," http://www.mugglenet.com/2004/08/the-north-tower-wands-and-where-to-find-them/). She suggests that Hagrid's umbrella contains not his own broken wand, but Moaning Myrtle's entirely intact wand—given that she would have had no more use of it at exactly the moment when Hagrid's was snapped. It can't be proven one way or the other unless Jo says so, but I'm fond of the theory.
[21] We don't know Grubbly-Plank's house, but a commitment to teaching regardless of politics suggests Ravenclaw.

> "You will find that I will only *truly* have left this school when none here are loyal to me. You will also find that help will always be given at Hogwarts to those who ask for it." (CS263-264)

At first glance, Dumbledore's promise of help to those who are loyal to him appears to be mysterious and abstract; how does one measure loyalty from afar? But there is a rational explanation, courtesy of online commenter GumWrappersAreLove1:

> I think [Dumbledore] might be referring to the Deluminator. [...] What if when Dumbledore said "none here are loyal to me" he was implying "none who love me speak my name"?! That would mean if Dumbledore had had the Deluminator with him when he was on his way to McGonagall's office to console the Weasleys, he would have heard Harry saying his name in the Chamber of Secrets. [...] I think Dumbledore heard Harry's voice, knew he was alive and fighting to save Ginny in the Chamber, and might have sent Fawkes.[22]

Later on in this book, we will discuss Dumbledore's issues with loyalty from others, but suffice to say he prizes it highly. It is absolutely in character for him to codify that into a spell or magical artifact.

What we know of the Deluminator from Ron's use of it in *Deathly Hallows* is that the wielder is able to hear when certain people speak his name. This would be a perfect way for Dumbledore to be at the ready

---

[22]Part of the discussion on Alohomora! Episode #251 (which I was a guest on). http://alohomorapodcast.com/episode-251-dh-7-revisit-kissing-advice/#comment-4024385833

should Harry ever need his immediate help: Dumbledore would just wait for his name to be invoked. A close read of *Chamber of Secrets* backs this up: Harry does not say Dumbledore's name between his sacking and the showdown in the Chamber of Secrets.[23]

To clarify, we don't know if Dumbledore was using the Deluminator for this purpose, or if it's an independent spell that he later put on the Deluminator specifically for Ron. But we can surmise that enchanting names in this fashion is very advanced magic: the only characters we know of who do so are Dumbledore and Voldemort (with the Taboo in *Deathly Hallows*).

If we reread the climax of *Chamber of Secrets* with this in mind, a whole lot of things begin to make sense. Harry first uses Dumbledore's name when he says to Riddle, "I bet Dumbledore saw right through you." (CS312) This was the moment that Dumbledore was alerted to what was going on, and began paying attention to the proceedings.

We don't know how much one can listen to once this magic is activated by the name, but in DH Ron hears Hermione talking about wands after she says his name. So one can listen to at least some conversation after the name. This may explain why Dumbledore is so seemingly omniscient in the post-battle meeting.

---

[23] This also explains why Dumbledore was unable to come to Harry's rescue in the graveyard in *Goblet of Fire*. Even if Dumbledore was once again using this spell during the Third Task, Voldemort is the only one to say his name during the proceedings (many times, in fact, during his monologue to the Death Eaters). As GumWrappersAreLove1 put it, "Harry doesn't say Dumbledore's name (or much of anything) in the Little Hangleton graveyard. I wouldn't be surprised if Dumbledore was anxiously fingering the Deluminator in his pocket while Harry was in the maze."

> "What interests *me* most," said Dumbledore gently, "is how Lord Voldemort managed to enchant Ginny, when my sources tell me he is currently in hiding in the forests of Albania." (CS328)

Dumbledore knows that it was Voldemort and that Ginny was enchanted because shortly after Harry first shouted about Dumbledore, Riddle explains how he manipulated Ginny. After the full and boastful confession, "Voldemort," said Riddle softly, "is my past, present, and future." (CS313)

Dumbledore is now paying very close attention, while Riddle speaks calmly. The second time Harry uses Dumbledore's name, Dumbledore hears Riddle getting agitated, so he sends Fawkes as backup.

> "Sorry to disappoint you and all that, but the greatest wizard in the world is Albus Dumbledore. Everyone says so. Even when you were strong, you didn't dare try and take over at Hogwarts. Dumbledore saw through you when you were at school and he still frightens you now, wherever you're hiding these days—"
>
> The smile had gone from Riddle's face, to be replaced by a very ugly look.
>
> "Dumbledore's been driven out of this castle by the mere memory of me!" he hissed.
>
> "He's not as gone as you might think!" Harry retorted. He was speaking at random, wanting to scare Riddle, wishing rather than believing it to be true.
>
> Riddle opened his mouth, but froze.

> Music was coming from somewhere. (CS314-315)

Why didn't Dumbledore come himself? This would be around the time Dumbledore had to deal with the distraught Weasleys, so he delegated the task to Fawkes. He fervently hopes that Harry and Fawkes together will be up to the task of defeating Riddle.

In Dumbledore's own words, Harry "acquitted [himself] beyond my wildest dreams." (OP838) Dumbledore is reinstated and gets to stick it to Lucius Malfoy, who's sacked from the Hogwarts Board of Governors. This moment is also the biggest success in Dumbledore's campaign to remove Lucius from being Lord Voldemort's Favorite Death Eater, since Voldemort's "anger was terrible to behold" (HBP508) when he found out Lucius had gotten the diary destroyed. Dumbledore also finds out how loyal Harry is to him. This is the beginning of Dumbledore caring more for Harry than for an ordinary student, because he's touched by Harry's faith.

Dumbledore has a very significant conversation with Harry after the incident. He withholds a crucial piece of information about the prophecy: "You were still so young, you see, and I could not find it in myself to spoil that night of triumph. . ." (OP838) He also receives a vital piece of information, one that leads us to ask a crucial question that we will revisit throughout this book.

What Did Dumbledore Know of Horcruxes?

By the time Harry is let in on the Horcrux hunt in *Half-Blood Prince* (and the reader with him), Dumbledore seems to have everything together. He knows what the Horcruxes are and how many there are. He's also collected all the necessary memories, and it's just a matter of telling Harry about it and then destroying them. At first, we do not question this; we're used to Dumbledore's seeming omniscience, so why wouldn't he have all the necessary information already? Even Lord Voldemort reinforces the idea: "You are omniscient as ever, Dumbledore." (HBP445)

But then, someone has to ask the very pertinent question: if Dumbledore has known all along about the Horcruxes, why did he only start hunting them in 1996? (The exact timing will be discussed in the Year 5 section.) He had years and years before that during which he could have hunted Horcruxes unmolested!

I believe the correct answer is the most straightforward one: Dumbledore did not know everything about everything until just before we did. So let us explore what Dumbledore knew and when—a recurring question to keep in mind in order to maintain a sense of perspective.

1992 and Earlier

Up until that very significant conversation in *Chamber of Secrets*, Dumbledore did not even know whether Voldemort had created Horcruxes or not. It may seem obvious in retrospect that he had. But consider this very telling line from Voldemort's monologue in *Goblet of Fire*: ". . . it appeared that one or more of my experiments had worked . . . for I had not been killed." (GF653) That means that Voldemort had made several "experiments" in his quest for immortality. How was Dumbledore to know what Dark magic Voldemort had performed? All Dumbledore knows is that Voldemort spent about twenty years exploring ways to become immortal, and Merlin knows which one he actually chose.

But suppose Dumbledore realized that Voldemort might have made a Horcrux. Dumbledore would not know that Voldemort made more than one because doing so is completely unprecedented. He tells Harry, "[Voldemort] was referring to his Horcruxes, Horcruxes in the plural, Harry, which I do not believe any other wizard has ever had." (HBP501-502) Just think of how horrified Slughorn is at Tom Riddle's suggestion of multiple Horcruxes in that crucial recovered memory (HBP498). If Dumbledore was contemplating different methods of immortality, I don't think he would consider multiple Horcruxes.

Let's say for argument's sake he suspects that Voldemort made one Horcrux. The only one he reasonably could have found, with the information available to him, is the locket or the ring. If Dumbledore suspected that the cup or the diary was the Horcrux, he would be at a complete dead end, since he can't exactly go snooping through the possessions of all the former Death Eaters.

So Dumbledore might suspect that there's one Horcrux out there. Having been collecting memories about Voldemort already, there are several possible candidates, but Dumbledore has no way of knowing which one is the Horcrux or where it will be found. Dumbledore is not even sure whether Voldemort has a Horcrux or if he used some other Dark magic. But with Voldemort temporarily out of the picture, Dumbledore can focus on other endeavors: rebuilding the world after the first Voldemort War, enacting his scheme surrounding the Sorcerer's Stone, and dealing with the Chamber of Secrets.

End of *Chamber of Secrets*

The first breakthrough comes at the end of *Chamber of Secrets*, when Harry comes into Dumbledore's office, triumphantly wielding a sword and a destroyed diary, telling strange tales of meeting a teenaged Voldemort. Dumbledore explains his thought process to Harry during their Horcruxes 101 lesson.

> "I was almost sure of it. The diary had been a Horcrux. But this raised as many questions as it answered.
>
> "What intrigued and alarmed me most was that that diary had been intended as a weapon as much as a safeguard."
>
> [. . .]
>
> "The careless way in which Voldemort regarded this Horcrux seemed most ominous to me. It suggested that he must have made— or been planning to make—more Horcruxes, so that the loss of his first would not be so detrimental." (HBP500-501)

Dumbledore gets confirmation that Voldemort did indeed make a Horcrux, but alarm bells go off in his head. If Voldemort treated his Horcrux as expendable, that means that Voldemort must have made more than one. This is a mind-blowing idea, but it appears to make sense. So now Dumbledore starts thinking, *Just how bad is the situation? Did Voldemort make two Horcruxes (unprecedented!), or did he go even further than that and make three?* The answer to "not who, but how?" is even more important than anyone initially thought.

While this is all quite frightening to contemplate, Dumbledore is not particularly frantic just yet. Voldemort is still somewhere in Albania, alone and almost powerless. The Sorcerer's Stone is destroyed, one Horcrux—Tom Riddle's Diary—is down, and things are looking rosy for the moment. I'm sure Dumbledore starts poring over his memories of Tom Riddle, doing his research, trying to identify what could possibly be a Horcrux.

However, this is all soon driven from his mind, and Horcruxes are put on the backburner for two years. Because if Dumbledore was hoping for some down time after the whole Chamber of Secrets debacle, he's about to get some really unwelcome news about a prisoner in Azkaban.

Chapter 3:
Albus Dumbledore and the Prisoner of Azkaban

Prisoner of Azkaban is a unique book among the seven for many reasons, chief among them the absence of Voldemort. It is also unique because it's the only book where the reader is pretty much on the same page as Dumbledore for most of it—believing in Sirius Black's guilt and at a loss as to how Sirius is achieving things.

Prisoner is also where Dumbledore's choice of D.A.D.A. professors begins to inform the story. Some context: Voldemort cursed the position when he applied for it and was rejected, which can be placed with reasonable certainty in the winter of the 1956-1957 schoolyear. (See Appendix A.) Let us take Dumbledore's statement at face value, that they "have never been able to keep a Defense Against the Dark Arts teacher for longer than a year since [Dumbledore] refused the post to Lord Voldemort." (HBP446)[24] That would mean Lockhart had been the thirty-fifth D.A.D.A. teacher in as many years.

As Lockhart's appointment indicates, Dumbledore has utterly exhausted the pool of potential job applicants who would actually be appointed purely for their pedagogical prowess. His appointments henceforth will be informed by ulterior motives. With Lupin, it's two-fold. On the one hand, Dumbledore

---

[24] Some argue that the language in *Sorcerer's Stone* indicates Quirrell had already been the D.A.D.A. professor before Harry's first year, including the fine folks over at *The Harry Potter Lexicon*, but I'll take the path of least resistance and assume Dumbledore accurately described the effects of the curse.

wants to help Lupin after Umbridge's anti-werewolf legislation makes it impossible for him to find work (OP302). On the other hand, it'll be mighty handy having one of Sirius's old best friends on hand, so Dumbledore can consult him about his former friend.

Unfortunately for Dumbledore, Lupin is not as forthcoming about Sirius as one would hope. Lupin does not tell Dumbledore the most crucial bit of information: that Sirius is an Animagus. Why? Lupin confesses, "It would have meant admitting that I'd betrayed his trust while I was at school, admitting that I'd led others along with me... and Dumbledore's trust has meant everything to me." (PA356)

But Dumbledore gets something even better out of Lupin's appointment: Lupin's mentorship of Harry. In this, Lupin acquits himself stupendously, teaching Harry Defense Against Dark Arts and reining in his more reckless impulses.

Dumbledore would have loved to keep Lupin around for another year, but he knows he cannot because of the curse. When Lupin hands in his resignation at the end of the year, Dumbledore somberly accepts it—a sharp contrast to his refusal of Hagrid's resignation half a year later.

Dumbledore's actions throughout Harry's third year don't really need explaining, until the fateful events of June 6, 1994. By examining what occurs that night, we not only get a further feel for how Dumbledore operates, we also examine his evolving relationship with two people: Harry and Snape.

The Matter of Buckbeak

When looking at the climaxes of the Harry Potter books, this is the one that I believe has generated more discussion than any other. It takes up a full quarter of the entire book and is largely viewed as the point where the series grew up. Many essays have been written about Dumbledore's seeming omniscience at the end of *Prisoner of Azkaban*. Fans theorized that maybe Dumbledore has a Time Turner of his own, which allows him to go back in time to tell himself things, which is a big headache for all of us.

I do not subscribe to this Time Turner theory (nor am I a fan of the "everyone has a Time Turner" gimmick used in Cursed Child). I think that everything in *Prisoner of Azkaban* can be explained by Dumbledore just being incredibly clever and always thinking many steps ahead.

First, let us look at Buckbeak's would-be execution. Dumbledore decides to join Hagrid for Buckbeak's execution, he "said he wants ter—ter be with [Hagrid]." (PA328) Is Dumbledore already scheming to send Harry and Hermione back in time to rescue Buckbeak? No. I think that Dumbledore really did want to comfort Hagrid. But also, Dumbledore probably thought that if there were a way to save Buckbeak, it would help for him to be onsite.

Once the Ministry officials arrive at Hagrid's hut, Dumbledore does not do anything at first, other than watch the proceedings. But then Dumbledore begins stalling for time just as Harry and Hermione are freeing Buckbeak.

> "One moment, please, Macnair," came Dumbledore's voice. "You need to sign too." The footsteps stopped. Harry heaved on the rope. Buckbeak snapped his beak and walked a little faster. [. . .] Harry could still hear Dumbledore's voice talking from within the cabin. (PA401)

Does Dumbledore know what it going on? Not necessarily. He does not need to.[25] He knows that there is a certain trio of students who care very much about Hagrid and who have an Invisibility Cloak. He knows that if there were an attempted rescue of Buckbeak, it would have to happen in the short interval between Macnair seeing Buckbeak tied up and all the paperwork being filled out. Therefore, it's just good sense to delay things a bit and give any would-be rescuers an additional bit of time. So Dumbledore stalls for time, just in case. And what do you know, he was right to do so!

> "Where is it?" said the reedy voice of the Committee member. "Where is the beast?"
>
> "It was tied here!" said the executioner furiously. "I saw it! Just here!"
>
> "How extraordinary," said Dumbledore. There was a note of amusement in his voice.
>
> [. . .]
>
> "Someone untied him!" the executioner was snarling. "We should search the grounds, the forest—"
>
> "Macnair, if Buckbeak has indeed been stolen, do you really think the thief will have led him away on foot?" said Dumbledore, still sounding amused. "Search the skies, if you will. . . . Hagrid, I could do with a cup of tea. Or a large brandy." (PA402)

---

[25] It is possible that he does know, due to either performing *Homenum Revelio*, or even just seeing Harry outside Hagrid's Hut (though I find the latter option unlikely). However, his behavior makes sense even if he doesn't know, but merely supposes.

To Harry, and to readers who believe in Dumbledore's omniscience, this certainly looks like Dumbledore knows everything that's going on. Why else isn't he surprised? How else would he know to badly advise Macnair to "search the skies"?

Because Dumbledore is exceedingly clever, and a master of deductive reasoning. To reiterate, he knows there are three students with an Invisibility Cloak who would very much want to free Buckbeak and who are the adventurous sort that would attempt to do so. It's not difficult to deduce that the Trio managed to free Buckbeak in the time that Dumbledore bought them.

Dumbledore is also relying on the Ministry's stupidity here. In fact, Dumbledore relies on this a lot that evening and later in the series as well; he will later deride the idea that "Harry and Hermione are able to be in two places at once" (PA420) in front of the Minister of Magic, assuming correctly that Fudge would not consider the possibility of Time Turner use. If one thinks about it, no thief in his right mind would try to fly away on Buckbeak right after stealing him. The execution was to take place "at sunset," (PA325) so one could still see in the twilight. There is almost no chance that a hippogriff could fly fast enough to be out of the field of vision in a minute.

Therefore, the logical conclusion is that Buckbeak was led away on foot. Dumbledore realizes this and banks on the Ministry officials not thinking it through. In their minds, of course a thief would fly away on a stolen flying animal. Dumbledore also realizes that Buckbeak would not be covered by the Invisibility Cloak and is likely still close by. He therefore hurries to get Macnair and company back inside Hagrid's hut to give Buckbeak's saviors more time to get away.

This is such classic Dumbledore! He is certainly having a lot of fun here. In fact, Dumbledore often seems to derive great pleasure in making a mockery of people he dislikes, which we'll see later in this very chapter with Snape and repeated throughout the series. Dumbledore keeps Fudge and Macnair occupied for the evening, and then all hell starts breaking loose two hours later.

Dumbledore is running around dealing with Sirius and Snape and all the ensuing mayhem. What does he know about Buckbeak? He knows that Buckbeak managed to escape. He knows that the Trio are the most likely candidates to be Buckbeak's rescuers; in fact, who else would do it? But the Trio has made no mention of Buckbeak, the timing does not really line up, and where on earth is Buckbeak now?

Dumbledore is also trying to figure out a way to get Sirius out of Hogwarts safely and quickly. Apparition does not work. There is likely a guard outside Flitwick's office, so if one were to get to Sirius inconspicuously, it would have to be through the window. There is also no time, so he will have to rely on Hermione's Time Turner. Dumbledore puts two and two together the way only he can and realizes that he has two refugees on his hands, one of whom can fly. He realizes that if the Trio currently in the hospital wing did not rescue Buckbeak, maybe that is because the time-travelling version did. And that is how he comes up with his brilliant plan to have Sirius escape on Buckbeak and gives Hermione the slightest of nudges: "You will be able to save more than one innocent life tonight." (PA393)

Coming Up With the Plan

There are two other possibilities for how Dumbledore thought of the plan to rescue Sirius and Buckbeak by using Hermione's Time Turner, aside from relying solely on his innate brilliance.

The first possibility: that Dumbledore actually sees the time-traveling Harry and Hermione flying on

THE LIFE AND LIES OF ALBUS DUMBLEDORE

Buckbeak. The timing is such that it could work. We are given three facts:

- Flitwick's office is not too far from the West Tower (from whence the time-traveling Harry and Hermione run back to the Hospital Wing)
- Dumbledore arrives at the Hospital Wing one or two minutes before the time-traveling begins.
- Dumbledore had "just been talking to Sirius Black" (PA390) when he arrives.

This means that Dumbledore would be finishing his interview with Sirius moments before Harry and Hermione fly in to rescue him. It is possible that Dumbledore saw Harry and Hermione flying by in one of the windows on the thirteenth floor, but knowing that Harry and Hermione are also in the Hospital Wing, he realizes that there must be time travel involved in rescuing Buckbeak and Sirius.

The second possibility relies on some more conjecture: that Dumbledore utilizes the Deluminator magic we discussed in Chapter 2 with some regularity, such as on evenings when he suspects Harry will be going on an adventure to save a hippogriff. Assuming the magic will pick up on all Harrys present at a moment in time who say Dumbledore's name, this is what Dumbledore would hear shortly before Buckbeak's execution:

> "Dumbledore just said—just said we could save more than one innocent life...." And then it hit him. "Hermione, we're going to save Buckbeak!"
>
> "But—how will that help Sirius?"
>
> "Dumbledore said—he just told us where the

> window is—the window of Flitwick's office! Where they've got Sirius locked up! We've got to fly Buckbeak up to the window and rescue Sirius! Sirius can escape on Buckbeak—they can escape together!" (PA396)

Of course, the mention of Sirius would lead Dumbledore to be concerned and confused when he first hears it. He may even have thought the magic was malfunctioning. And Harry does not say Dumbledore's name during the entire Shrieking Shack scene, so that's no help at all.

But once Dumbledore spoke to Sirius and understood that Harry and Hermione believed his innocence, then he would remember the weird conversation he'd overheard, and realize that he had already heard what his plan was going to be!

These two possibilities are not mutually exclusive—either, neither, or both could be true. It does not have much bearing on the story either way, but it is entertaining to consider the possibilities that open up when Dumbledore gets involved in time travel.

Dumbledore Deploys Harry

It's worth noting how Dumbledore's treatment of Harry and his friends is slowly changing. Dumbledore is now entrusting important missions to the Trio, missions where a man's life hangs in the balance. This is a far cry from the micro-managed controlled experiment of *Sorcerer's Stone*. If we read closely, we can continue to see Dumbledore's burgeoning affection for and trust in Harry throughout the series.

If it still seems ludicrous to entrust these kinds of missions to thirteen-year-olds, one can look to Dumbledore's background for an explanation. Albus's father, Percival Dumbledore, was incarcerated when

Albus was around eleven, which would have made Albus (the oldest sibling) the "man of the house." This independence and responsibility at a young age may have skewed Dumbledore's perspective on what an appropriate amount of responsibility is for a young teenager.

In an echo of things to come, Dumbledore gives Harry and Hermione the bare minimum of required information to proceed—if we're being charitable, we can say in this instance it's because Dumbledore is wary of messing with time. And there is another key aspect of Dumbledore's scheme in *Prisoner of Azkaban* that will echo in *Deathly Hallows*: he entrusts Hermione to be a moderating influence on Harry.

> "What we need," said Dumbledore slowly, and his light blue eyes moved from Harry to Hermione, "is more time."
>
> [...]
>
> "But remember this, both of you: you must not be seen. Miss Granger, you know the law—you know what is at stake...." (PA393)

Dumbledore realizes that Harry is far too emotional at the moment. He knows that Harry has a reckless Gryffindor streak, which we see on display when Harry wheedles Hermione to snatch the Invisibility Cloak or Wormtail and change time. Meanwhile, he knows that Hermione has a higher regard for the law, and a cooler head on her shoulders—she'll be able to keep Harry in check, give or take one impressive stag Patronus. Dumbledore's plan in *Sorcerer's Stone*, to give the Trio experience working as a team to perform dangerous tasks, has borne fruit, and he believes Hermione is up to the challenge. So Hermione gets to lead the mission.

Either way, Dumbledore has sent Harry and Hermione off into the past to save the future and turns around to see Harry breathlessly say, "We did it! Sirius has gone, on Buckbeak...." (PA418) Dumbledore's plan succeeded! There's just one loose end... Severus Snape.

Snape's Anger

Thus far, I have avoided discussing Severus Snape, as there are entire books wholly devoted to the Potions Master. However, Snape is now unavoidable, because Dumbledore's relationship with him proves key to much of the story.

Snape is in a towering rage for much of the night, which is unusual for him. While he is never happy, he usually maintains his composure, even when fireworks are set off in his class or when someone literally sets fire to him. So when he makes a dramatic entrance in the Shrieking Shack, we must consider what is going on. Of course, it all comes back to something Dumbledore did or did not do.

When Hermione implores Snape to hear Sirius out, instead of the usual cutting remark, he goes into CapsLock mode (giving us, in fact, the first instance of CapsLock in the series).

> "KEEP QUIET, YOU STUPID GIRL!" Snape shouted, looking suddenly quite deranged. "DON'T TALK ABOUT WHAT YOU DON'T UNDERSTAND!" (PA360)

Jo is always deliberate in her choice of words. Her word choice gives us a subconscious cue that Snape is the villain in this scene, because his language ("you stupid girl") echoes Voldemort's language from Harry's dementor-induced flashbacks: "Stand aside, you silly girl..." (PA179)[26]

Snape may be many things, but he had never been described as deranged before. In fact, he never shouts, since he has "the gift of keeping a class silent without trying." (SS136-137) However, in this scene, "there was a mad glint in Snape's eyes that Harry had never seen before. He seemed beyond reason." (PA360) Upon further provocation, Snape gets even crazier.

> "SILENCE! I WILL NOT BE SPOKEN TO LIKE THAT!" Snape shrieked, looking madder than ever. "Like father, like son, Potter! . . . You would have been well served if he'd killed you! You'd have died like your father, too arrogant to believe you might be mistaken in Black— now get out of the way, or I will make you. GET OUT OF THE WAY POTTER!" (PA361)

Snape says some pretty awful things to Harry over the course of six years, but never that Harry should have been killed... In fact, Snape's only reason for living these days is to ensure that Harry isn't killed.

But in the context of "The Prince's Tale," it makes sense. Snape says James died because he was "too arrogant to believe [he] might be mistaken in Black." And who else died because of James's perceived arrogance? Lily, Snape's only love.

Snape blames Sirius for causing Lily's death by his supposed betrayal, which is a huge factor in Snape acting so unhinged. Snape wants revenge on Sirius for

---

[26] Credit for this brilliant catch goes to Daniela Teo in The Two-Way Mirror #10: "The Triwizard Tasks and the Seven Books," http://www.mugglenet.com/2004/12/the-two-way-mirror-10-the-triwizard-tasks-and-the-seven-books/.

Lily's death. And he is livid that Harry is repeating his father's mistakes by trusting Sirius.

For many years, I assumed that was all there was to it. But in *SNAPE: A Definite Reading*, Lorrie Kim makes a great argument that Snape was traumatized by The Prank. When he looks "quite deranged," Lorrie attributes it to him "entering a state of post-traumatic flashback." (p. 71) And that is what eventually leads to a big mess for Albus Dumbledore—but one that, rather like the Lucius Malfoy debacle, Dumbledore inadvertently brought upon himself with his anti-Slytherin bias.

The Prank

During the Marauders' fifth year, there was an incident where Sirius attempted to play a prank on Snape. In Lupin's words:

> "Severus was very interested in where I went every month. [. . .] Snape had seen me crossing the grounds with Madam Pomfrey one evening as she led me toward the Whomping Willow to transform. Sirius thought it would be—er—amusing, to tell Snape all he had to do was prod the knot on the tree trunk with a long stick, and he'd be able to get in after me. Well, of course, Snape tried it—if he'd got as far as this house, he'd have met a fully grown werewolf—but your father, who'd heard what Sirius had done, went after Snape and pulled him back, at great risk to his life . . . Snape glimpsed me, though, at the end of the tunnel. He was forbidden by Dumbledore to tell anybody, but from that time on he knew what I was. . . ." (PA357)

Snape, as he tells it, seems to agree with most of the facts.

> "Your saintly father and his friends played a highly amusing joke on me that would have resulted in my death if your father hadn't got cold feet at the last moment. There was nothing brave about what he did. He was saving his own skin as much as mine. Had their joke succeeded, he would have been expelled from Hogwarts." (PA285)

Snape believes that if he had actually been killed or turned into a werewolf, the Marauders would have been expelled. But attempted murder only gets a slap on the wrist for Sirius.

The fandom's perception of The Prank has undergone a fascinating evolution of late. It was almost a decade after DH was published that a majority of fans came around to realizing that what Sirius did was absolutely not okay. He should have received a major punishment—instead, any punishment he received was mild enough to not even merit a mention in the narrative, presumably no more than lots of detentions.

Rather, it's Severus who was punished with a gag order, forbidding him from telling anyone about what happened. It should not be understated how much of a profound impact this would have had on teenaged Snape, especially occurring no more than half a year before his break with Lily. The champion of the fight against Voldemort, a beacon of virtue for the "good side," just showed that he did not care about an attempt on Snape's life.

What was Dumbledore thinking? Taking the less charitable view, this could just be another entry in a long list of instances of Dumbledore siding with

Gryffindors over Slytherins. More charitably, if one does not consider the historical context, we could attribute it solely to Dumbledore's tendency to give people second chances.

Unfortunately, awarding Sirius a second chance robbed Severus Snape of his first chance. The Prank is doubtless one of the main factors that drew Snape to the Dark side. After his falling out with Lily (and it's no surprise his nerves were on edge that following June), he had no one to turn to except his fellow Slytherins. He could justify it to himself by claiming that the other side was just as bad, as evidenced by Sirius and Dumbledore's disregard for his life.

But none of this is happening in a vacuum: Dumbledore knows Sirius's family background, and Sirius's reckless and ruthless temperament. Especially in the middle of Voldemort's reign of terror, it would be all too easy for Sirius to return to his roots and join the Dark side if he were removed from the moderating influence of the Marauders. Given that Sirius is a wizard of prodigious skill, Dumbledore does not want to risk it.

The unwritten story of The Prank is Dumbledore, in the thick of the first Voldemort War, making the kind of calculated decisions he would have to make later on in the HP book series. He is caught in a zero-sum quandary between Snape and Sirius. Whoever he sides with, there is a substantial possibility the other one will seethe right into Voldemort's arms. Sirius and Snape both have awful home lives, an astounding level of magical skill, a certain lack of empathy, and Gryffindors as a moderating influence. So who's Dumbledore to bet on?

After weighing the options, Dumbledore bets on Sirius. For all that Sirius is rough around the edges, and just displayed an alarming murderous tendency, he is still a Gryffindor. He still spends his time surrounded by good people, who will presumably impress upon him the severity of what he just did. (Remus, I imagine, was none too pleased at being weaponized by Sirius.) Sirius could still become a promising member of the Order of the Phoenix.

Is fifth year too early for Dumbledore to be thinking of recruitment for the Order? Most of the adults we see seem eager to mollycoddle Harry and his peers when they are sixteen. But in the 1970s, Dumbledore would have been desperate. Lupin tells Molly about his time in the first Order of the Phoenix: "We were outnumbered twenty to one by the Death Eaters and they were picking us off one by one...." (OP177) And that chilling statement comes from Lupin, who was one of five young wizards and witches who joined the Order late in the game. Before the Marauders and Lily joined, the Order would have been even more hopelessly outgunned. Dumbledore would have been desperate for new recruits, desperate enough to look among his student body.

He sees promising young recruits among the Marauders. Dumbledore may also have factored in that losing Sirius would have altered the entire group in an unfavorable way—for all that Dumbledore is a solitary person, he is very well attuned to group dynamics. We see how he groomed the Trio to be a cohesive asset; he may have intended the same with the Marauders.

And on the other side, he sees young Severus.

> "Snape's always been fascinated by the Dark Arts, he was famous for it at school. [. . .] Snape knew more curses when he arrived at school than half the kids in seventh year, and he was part of a gang of Slytherins who nearly all turned out to be Death Eaters." (GF531)

Dumbledore is essentially profiling Snape and the Marauders, and this is a perfect example of how profiling can be a self-fulfilling prophecy. On the one hand, there is a promising group of young Gryffindors who will most likely become valuable assets for the Order of the Phoenix. On the other hand, there is one boy immersed in a toxic environment of Slytherins—up to his greasy hair in Dark Arts and hanging out with the likes of Rosier and Lestrange. For Dumbledore, it's a no-brainer: bet on Sirius by showing him clemency, and hope for the best with Severus. Perhaps he hoped Lily would have been able to salvage Severus. And no doubt he made Sirius feel about an inch tall with a thorough guilt trip when he allowed Sirius to remain at Hogwarts.

One thing is very clear: Dumbledore failed teenaged Snape very badly. He made a very difficult choice and sided with the Gryffindor over the Slytherin—as he always seems to do.

One wonders whether Dumbledore is aware of his own biases or if he always justifies them somehow? In the Tom Riddle/Hagrid episode, Dumbledore kept a shaky moral high ground because of Riddle's culpability in Myrtle's murder. In the Snape/Marauder episode, it was all about the war effort. And in the case of his mistreatment of Harry's Slytherin peers, maybe it's all done for Harry's benefit... but that reasoning is rather flimsy.

We are shown later that Dumbledore is aware of it, as he is very self-aware in general. And if that choice of Dumbledore's is indeed what cemented Sirius and Snape's allegiances in the first Voldemort War, it is one of the most momentous decisions he makes in terms of how far-reaching the consequences are.

That choice is what informed Snape's reactions on that fateful June evening, eighteen years later. Once again, Dumbledore sides against Snape... once again, to his peril.

The Parting of Ways

"The Prince's Tale" shows us the progression of the exceedingly complex relationship between Albus Dumbledore and Severus Snape. However, there are gaps in "The Prince's Tale," accounting for most of Harry's first five years at Hogwarts. As we know, just because parts of the plot happen off-screen, it does not mean that they are not significant. In fact, in that gap we find a fascinating evolution of Snape's relationship with Dumbledore... starting with that fateful night in *Prisoner of Azkaban*, when everyone's emotions were running very high.

For a whole host of reasons, Snape is on edge the whole night. He "snarled" at Dumbledore and yelled, "Miss Granger, HOLD YOUR TONGUE!" all in front of the Minister of Magic (PA390). Snape does not usually disrespect Dumbledore in public, nor is he as awful to his students when witnesses are around. He's not acting wholly rationally, but he grows infinitely more unhinged when Sirius escapes.

> "HE DIDN'T DISAPPARATE!" Snape roared, now very close at hand. "YOU CAN'T APPARATE OR DISAPPARATE INSIDE THIS CASTLE! THIS—HAS—SOMETHING—TO—DO—WITH—POTTER!"
>
> [...]
>
> Fudge, Snape, and Dumbledore came striding into the ward. Dumbledore alone looked calm. Indeed, he looked as though he was quite enjoying himself. Fudge appeared angry. But Snape was beside himself.
>
> "OUT WITH IT, POTTER!" he bellowed. "WHAT DID YOU DO?"

> [...]
>
> "See here, Snape, be reasonable," said Fudge. "This door's been locked, we just saw—"
>
> "THEY HELPED HIM ESCAPE, I KNOW IT!" Snape howled, pointing at Ron and Hermione. His face was twisted; spit was flying from his mouth.
>
> "Calm down, man!" Fudge barked. "You're talking nonsense!"
>
> "YOU DON'T KNOW POTTER!" shrieked Snape. "HE DID IT, I KNOW HE DID IT—"
>
> "That will do, Severus," said Dumbledore quietly. "Think about what you are saying. This door has been locked since I left the ward ten minutes ago. Madam Pomfrey, have these students left their beds?"
>
> "Of course not!" said Madam Pomfrey, bristling. "I would have heard them!"
>
> "Well, there you have it, Severus," said Dumbledore calmly. "Unless you are suggesting that Harry and Hermione are able to be in two places at once, I'm afraid I don't see any point in troubling them further."
>
> Snape stood there, seething, staring from Fudge, who looked thoroughly shocked at his behavior, to Dumbledore, whose eyes were twinkling behind his glasses. Snape whirled about, robes swishing behind him, and stormed out of the ward. (PA419-420)

This is a fascinating passage to read, because our interpretation changes completely based on whether you believe Snape knows about Hermione's Time Turner. It could really be either one. Remember how Dumbledore relied on the Ministry's stupidity to help Buckbeak get away? He does this again, banking on Fudge not realizing Hermione might have a Time Turner. But why risk it?

If Snape knows about Hermione's Time Turner, then Dumbledore is sending Snape a discreet message: stop talking now! By mentioning time travel, which is quite obviously the answer Snape is seeking, Dumbledore would be saying to Snape that there is a lot going on Snape doesn't realize. Dumbledore would be banking on Snape obeying the unspoken command, and to be fair, Snape does desist immediately after this. There is much to recommend this view on the passage, but I am a detractor.

For me, the problem is that Dumbledore does not know that Snape will obey him. Snape is livid, for a host of reasons,[27] and it's pretty clear Snape has run amok when he starts yelling at the Minister of Magic. I don't think Dumbledore would trust Snape to be reasonable enough to shut up given a clue from Dumbledore. He would not risk giving Snape the answer to incriminating the Trio, given Snape's state of mind.

It's reasonable to expect Snape not to know that Hermione has a Time Turner. After all, I doubt he would care very much how Hermione maintains her academic schedule, and the only teacher confirmed to know about it is McGonagall. The whole Time Turner thing seems to be treated on a very need-to-know basis, given that Harry and Ron themselves don't need to know. This points to Dumbledore: Dumbledore

---

[27] To recap: He relived one of the worst nights of his life. He failed to get revenge on his childhood bully. He failed to avenge Lily's death. And he was foiled by his three least favorite students. All in all, not a good night for him.

probably realized early on that Harry's best friend having a Time Turner might come in handy, and all of Dumbledore's information concerning Harry and co. is distributed on a need-to-know basis. Snape likely did not need to know and therefore didn't. While Snape may have been aware of the existence of Time Turners in general, Dumbledore banked on Snape not connecting that to the situation at hand.

This echoes Dumbledore's earlier behavior with the Ministry. Just as he banked on being smarter than the Ministry officials, he is now hoping Snape isn't as clever as he is. And just as Dumbledore was amused when making a mockery of Macnair, he is now "quite enjoying himself" by seeing Snape goaded (PA419). And this is because Dumbledore is extremely disappointed in Severus Snape tonight.

Dumbledore was once full of "contempt" for Snape (DH677) but believed that Snape had redeemed himself. Over the last thirteen years, Dumbledore has worked with Snape, taken him into his confidences more than anyone else, and trusted Snape with the all-important task of protecting Harry. At this point, Dumbledore believes that Snape has become a decent person.

Then Snape completely shatters all of that in one night. In Dumbledore's view, Snape shows himself to be cruel, vindictive, and irrational. Snape is willing to sentence an innocent man to have his soul sucked out. Snape appears unconcerned with uncovering the truth, not bothering with finding out about Pettigrew in his haste to fulfill a vendetta. This is the man to whom Dumbledore entrusts Harry's wellbeing? Completely unacceptable.

When Snape continues this pattern of behavior, trying to pin the mess on Harry, Dumbledore does not like Snape at all in that moment. And when Dumbledore does not like someone, he quite enjoys goading them—in fact, I think most of the times we see

Dumbledore mentioned as enjoying himself, it's because he's taking the mickey out of the Dursleys or various Ministry people. So it is entirely in character for Dumbledore to have some fun at Snape's expense in this moment, just as he recently did with Macnair and Fudge.

Several very passionate MuggleNet commenters have pointed out that Snape's behavior is excusable based on his hearing only the part of the Marauders' story that focused on their school years and none of the later bits about Sirius's innocence and Pettigrew's guilt. While this exonerates Snape to us readers (to an extent), it's doubtful that Dumbledore was aware of this finer distinction. We have had years of rereading the passage to pick up on this. Dumbledore has only had a very emotional and hurried account from Sirius, an evidently biased account from Snape, and some disjointed yelling from Harry and Hermione. This is one of the very rare instances where we readers know more than Dumbledore. And as evidenced by the subsequent events I'm about to go into, Dumbledore is certainly unhappy with Snape, so this seems the most plausible line of reasoning.

What is striking is that the move to goad Snape might hurt Dumbledore's endgame. Dumbledore knows that Voldemort will rise again one day, and when that day comes, Snape would be an invaluable asset—he already made the mistake of losing Snape's allegiance once before. So what possesses Dumbledore to so antagonize Snape?

The answer is Harry, Dumbledore's big blind spot. Especially after the events in the *Chamber of Secrets*, Dumbledore has grown to care for Harry immensely. Harry is Dumbledore's weakness; he cares more for Harry's wellbeing than for the eventualities of war. He says, "What did I care if numbers of nameless and faceless people and creatures were slaughtered in the vague future, if in the here and now you were alive, and well, and happy?" (OP839) Therefore, Dumbledore was willing to antagonize Snape for Harry's happiness.

Having his godfather around would be the best possible thing for Harry's happiness. Dumbledore wants to have Sirius around to take care of Harry, to serve as a much-needed father figure. Dumbledore finally has a way of ensuring Harry's emotional wellbeing, so when Snape threatens that, Dumbledore is absolutely not having it. This is why Dumbledore, rather riskily, sides with Sirius over Snape, and Snape knows this.

This leads to an off-screen estrangement between Dumbledore and Snape. The following morning, Snape "accidentally let slip that [Remus] is a werewolf" at breakfast (PA423). Snape must surely have calmed down somewhat overnight, so this is a rational act of open defiance against Dumbledore. Snape knows how mad Dumbledore would be if Remus's secret got out—after all, Snape has been keeping it since he was sixteen.

This is very deliberate on Snape's part, proving that his mind is still lingering on The Prank. There are a thousand different ways he could have chosen to spite Dumbledore—indeed, we'll see some of them later on. But his opening blow is to do the one thing that Dumbledore forbade him from doing the first time Dumbledore sided with the Marauders over Snape: reveal that Lupin's a werewolf.

We have to wonder whether Snape and Dumbledore had a chat sometime between the hospital wing screaming match and breakfast, given that they were arguing in the hospital wing until after midnight. If they did, Snape was not satisfied, leading to his outing of Lupin in total disregard of Dumbledore's orders. It's also possible they didn't, because we have a tiny bit of evidence that Snape did not tell Dumbledore everything that transpired. When interrogating Crouch Jr. a year later, Dumbledore does not know about the

Marauder's Map: "Map? What map is this?" (GF690) Yet Snape knows about the Map, because not only is he present for Lupin's discussion of it (PA355), he also sees it in Lupin's office: "Lying on your desk was a certain map." (PA358)[28] It's possible Snape and Dumbledore talked and it didn't come up, but it seems likelier they were both in a huff and didn't talk that night.

So Snape outs Lupin. Dumbledore, meanwhile, acts even more drastically: he calls in a new right-hand man. No longer willing to rely on Snape, Dumbledore gets in touch with his old friend Alastor Moody over the summer and asks him to come to Hogwarts as the new D.A.D.A. teacher. Moody replaces Snape as the wizard Dumbledore can rely on to watch over Harry, and to help out with things. Sirius assumes Dumbledore called Moody in because Dumbledore is "reading the signs," (GF226), but I fail to see how the Dark Mark at the World Cup is much more worrying than notorious mass murderer Sirius Black coming after Harry the previous year. Moody isn't called in for extra protection; it's because Dumbledore no longer relies on Snape. And that leads to a very unpleasant year at Hogwarts for all involved.

---

[28] Credit for this brilliant observation goes to D.W. Hill, who wrote a riveting series of editorials about the Dumbledore/Snape relationship pre-DH,
http://www.mugglenet.com/2007/06/dumbledores-trust-in-snape-part-3-riffs-and-curiosities/.

Chapter 4:
Albus Dumbledore and the Goblet of Fire

Giving credit where it's due: Voldemort's plan in *Goblet of Fire* was brilliant. But first, let's focus on Dumbledore. In *Goblet of Fire*, for once, he is being outplayed by Voldemort. Between Trelawney's prophecy the previous year[29], the deaths of Bertha Jorkins and Frank Bryce, the Dark Mark at the World Cup, and then Harry's name coming out of the Goblet of Fire, Dumbledore knows that something is afoot and it probably has to do with Voldemort. He is extra vigilant in watching Harry and relies on his old friend Moody to do the same. And in the meantime, he wracks his brains trying to figure out who's behind all this.

I will not dive too deeply into his reasoning throughout the book, because I almost wholly agree with Josie Kearns's masterful essay, "A Very Bad Year for Albus Dumbledore."[30] The gist of it is that Dumbledore can narrow down the suspects to Bagman, Karkaroff, or something weird and magical going on. (After all, he just witnessed Pettigrew come back from being presumed dead, and as an Animagus, to boot—this certainly expands his lines of inquiry.) Dumbledore also knows that something weird is going

---

[29] "THE DARK LORD WILL RISE AGAIN WITH HIS SERVANT'S AID, GREATER AND MORE TERRIBLE THAN EVER HE WAS." (PA324)
[30] This is probably my favorite essay that I've ever read about the *Harry Potter* series; it completely opened my eyes to both the fact that Dumbledore is not always omniscient and the fact that his relationship with Snape is key.
https://hp-companion.com/essays/gfessay/

on with Mr. Crouch when he stops showing up to the Tournament, but what is it and what does it have to do with everything else?

Snape's Grudge

Dumbledore is trying to solve this whodunit at the same time as the Trio and the reader. However, in this instance Harry and the reader have more information than Dumbledore does, through interactions with the suspects. Consider some of the things we know that Dumbledore doesn't:

- Winky the house-elf was "saving Crouch a seat" at the Quidditch World Cup—for which he never showed. It is possible that Sirius relays this information after "Padfoot Returns"—but that is not until March.
- Bagman's offer to help Harry, or his odd appearance in the woods right after the Dark Mark appeared
- The entirety of "The Egg and The Eye" episode following Harry's bath in the prefects bathroom, where Harry sees "Bartemius Crouch" in Snape's office and invisibly observes a late-night run-in of Snape, Filch, and someone he thinks is Mad-Eye Moody

It is this last point that proves crucial. A careful read of the scene shows that the only reason Crouch Jr. is getting away with his schemes is because Snape and Dumbledore are no longer on speaking terms. Consider Snape's showdown with the imposter Moody after Harry's jaunt to the prefects' bathroom. "'Dumbledore happens to trust me!' said Snape through clenched teeth. 'I refuse to believe that he gave you orders to search my office!'" (GF472) This certainly sounds like

Snape is being defensive about a touchy subject—it hearkens back to how much Lupin prized Dumbledore's trust, and suggests that Snape valued it just as highly. This comment illustrates the breakdown of communication between Snape and Dumbledore. Of course Dumbledore gave no such order, and if Snape had but checked with Dumbledore, Crouch Jr.'s whole scheme would have unraveled.

In fact, Crouch Jr. comes to rely on this. During "The Madness of Mr. Crouch," he arrives on the scene very quickly and attributes this to "Snape said something about Crouch—" (GF561) Once again, if Dumbledore had mentioned this to Snape, Fake Moody would have been revealed as the culprit. But by this point, Crouch Jr. knows he can rely on the fact that the two are not talking.

The rift between Snape and Dumbledore lasts through the entirety of *Goblet of Fire*. And not only is Snape bitter and uncommunicative towards Dumbledore, he also truly reaches the zenith of his unpleasantness and cruelty in the fourth book. While he was never a nice guy, his actions in *Goblet of Fire* are beyond the pale. He threatens Harry with Veritaserum. He reads Rita Skeeter's humiliating article aloud in class—it's the kind of thing that would get any normal professor fired (GF515). And worst of all, he insults the appearance of a fifteen-year-old girl in front of all her peers (GF299-300). This hurt Hermione so much that she permanently changed her appearance by shrinking her teeth. Almost all of the evidence that Snape is a loathsome human being comes from *Goblet of Fire*, when he was acting out because he was angry with Dumbledore.

The only conversation we are aware of Snape and Dumbledore having in private this year is revealed in "The Prince's Tale," taking place right after the Yule Ball.

> "Well?" murmured Dumbledore.
>
> "Karkaroff's Mark is becoming darker too. He is panicking, he fears retribution; you know how much help he gave the Ministry after the Dark Lord fell." Snape looked sideways at Dumbledore's crooked-nosed profile. "Karkaroff intends to flee if the Mark burns."
>
> "Does he?" said Dumbledore softly, as Fleur Delacour and Roger Davies came giggling in from the grounds. "And are you tempted to join him?"
>
> "No," said Snape, his black eyes on Fleur's and Roger's retreating figures. "I am not such a coward." (DH679-680)

This passage can be read several ways, but I think the reading most consistent with the rest of the book is Snape and Dumbledore discussing business without any warmth and feeling out where their relationship stands. Half a year on from the Sirius Black debacle, Snape feels enough of a sense of duty to inform Dumbledore about the Dark Mark growing stronger, primarily because he has more animosity for Voldemort than for Dumbledore at the moment.

Tellingly, however, Dumbledore feels the need to question Snape's loyalties. He asks if Snape is tempted to join Karkaroff because that is a distinct possibility in Dumbledore's mind. Snape has shown that he puts his personal grudges above Harry's wellbeing. Dumbledore is aware that Snape will do almost anything out of vindictiveness. Thirteen years after Snape pledged his loyalty, Dumbledore needs to check in and see how far Snape is willing to take this conflict. This is a tacit acknowledgement of their estrangement by Dumbledore.

The next line from Dumbledore is the single most offensive thing he says: "You are a braver man by far than Igor Karkaroff. You know, I sometimes think we Sort too soon...." And with all but a mic drop, Dumbledore walks away. He implied that if any Slytherin exhibits bravery or other positive qualities, they're in the wrong house because no good people ever go to Slytherin.

Two layers exist here. First, Dumbledore is needling Snape; it's well-known that Snape appears to have a lot of Slytherin pride.[31] Second, Dumbledore is at his most candid when conversing with Snape, so this probably is an accurate reflection of Dumbledore's feelings, a capstone on half a century of blatant partisanship.

Did Snape ever consider defecting from Dumbledore's side during *Goblet of Fire*? It's an interesting question to ponder. If Snape had a third option to declare allegiance to, aside from Voldemort and Dumbledore, I believe he would have in a heartbeat. But much like American elections, he only had two real options, however unpalatable he might find them. And whatever slights he received from Dumbledore, whether recent or half a lifetime ago, nothing could make Snape return to Voldemort. A combination of obsessive love and an impressive ability to hold a grudge ensured that Snape would

---

[31] Lorrie Kim makes an intriguing point (SNAPE23) that Snape's partisanship towards Slytherins is his way of boosting them because they're ostracized for their connection to Voldemort and the Dark Arts. As is usual for her, it's a very charitable view of Snape. However, I posit that Snape favors the Slytherins and undermines the Gryffindors to counterbalance what he has observed to be Dumbledore's bias in the opposite direction. But as we witness in *Sorcerer's Stone*, once Harry enters the picture and gets Dumbledore more involved in Hogwarts, Snape's efforts prove futile.

never ever forgive Voldemort for Lily's death, and his vindictiveness ensured he would forever do whatever must be done to defeat Voldemort ... however much he may dislike his allies.

This conversation between Dumbledore and Snape also presents an interesting mirror to Voldemort and Wormtail's exchange later in GoF: "May your loyalty never waver again, Wormtail," said Voldemort. (GF650) Both Dumbledore and Voldemort are speaking to followers whose loyalty has wavered before, and who are in their current position due to a betrayal of his former master.

Dumbledore is much more diplomatic about it (questioning the servant's continued loyalty instead of demanding it). Yet both Dumbledore and Voldemort take the opportunity to needle Snape/Pettigrew. Dumbledore makes a dig about Slytherins. Voldemort throws in a deliciously ironic verbal slap, demanding loyalty and calling him "Wormtail" all in the same sentence, as a reminder of the childhood friends he betrayed.

But although Dumbledore is now assured that Snape's loyalty won't waver, their relationship deteriorates further, because by the end of May Snape seems to feel very little duty to Dumbledore at all.

> "Mr. Crouch!" Harry shouted. "From the Ministry! He's ill or something—he's in the forest, he wants to see Dumbledore! Just give me the password up to—"
>
> "The headmaster is busy, Potter," said Snape, his thin mouth curling into an unpleasant smile.
>
> "I've got to tell Dumbledore!" Harry yelled.
>
> "Didn't you hear me, Potter?"

THE LIFE AND LIES OF ALBUS DUMBLEDORE

> Harry could tell Snape was thoroughly enjoying himself, denying Harry the very thing he wanted when he was so panicky. (GF558)

Let's consider this. Snape has just run into a frantic Harry trying to get into Dumbledore's office. Harry yells that a vanished Ministry official has shown up on the Hogwarts grounds and is crazy, and this high-ranking crazy Ministry official is running amok with a Triwizard champion. Snape decides to completely disregard all of this for the simple joy of tormenting Harry for a little bit.

It's a rather interesting way to prioritize. Snape enjoys irking Harry, but he is intelligent enough to realize that if Harry is trying to see Dumbledore, there is a good reason, and that Dumbledore would be unhappy at Snape's interference. This is an act of deliberate defiance against Dumbledore by Snape, a full year after the events of *Prisoner of Azkaban*. It's Snape being petty. After all, no one holds a grudge quite like Snape.

All this serves to reinforce how angry Dumbledore must have been in *Prisoner* to risk drawing the ire of Snape—outing Lupin, obstructing Harry, and so on. Dumbledore reads people better than almost anyone, and he must know how vindictive Snape can be. Dumbledore is paying the price for not backing up Snape.

We get a final indication of how the two have grown apart during the Third Task. With the Crouch episode fresh in Dumbledore's mind, Snape is not even entrusted with patrolling the maze during the Task; that job is given to Moody, McGonagall, Hagrid, and Flitwick (GF620). This is a stark departure from how Dumbledore usually operates; even earlier that year, when Harry's name came out of the Goblet of Fire, it was McGonagall and Snape who accompanied

Dumbledore (GF275). Dumbledore no longer assigns Snape any crucial tasks, and from all we know of Snape, he must have perceived this as a slight.

However, as we've established, Snape's primary goal will always be revenge on Voldemort. This is why, once the imposter Moody is unmasked and Voldemort is revealed to have risen again, Dumbledore and Snape quickly reconcile. In fact, we witness this reconciliation without realizing it. Snape, in an uncharacteristic move, immediately brushes the grudge aside, backing up Dumbledore in pursuing Fake Moody and following Dumbledore's instructions with nary a snide comment (GF680). Dumbledore, realizing the major point of contention in their relationship, asks Sirius to come forward in Snape's presence; this is Dumbledore silently challenging Snape as to whether Snape can put aside his hatred of Sirius. And then Dumbledore says the words Snape has been waiting to hear all year: "I trust you both." (GF712) It is at this moment that Dumbledore and Snape are reconciled.

Mindful of this, Dumbledore's instructions to Snape are far politer than those for everyone else. He issues no-nonsense commands to everyone else, but to Snape he says, "Severus, you know what I must ask you to do. If you are ready ... if you are prepared ..." (GF713) Dumbledore is rarely so delicate in moments of action (consider his briskness when confronting Fake Moody or Fudge in the OotP climax), so this is noteworthy for showcasing their newly mended relationship.

We see their relationship is back to normal in *Order of the Phoenix*, because Snape actually accepts Dumbledore's assignment to teach Harry Occlumency. While the idea of humiliating Harry on a regular basis probably holds some appeal to Snape, spending additional time with Harry is not something Snape wants to do. If Dumbledore had asked Snape to teach Harry Occlumency in *Goblet of Fire*, I don't believe for a moment that Snape would have agreed ... nor do I believe Dumbledore would have asked.

But now Dumbledore trusts him enough to ask, and Snape attempts to oblige, until his and Harry's enmity proves too great. Note that Dumbledore does not appear to blame Snape for the "fiasco" (HBP79) of the Occlumency lessons. He either respects Snape for trying, or he just doesn't have the luxury of antagonizing Snape when it's crunch time against Voldemort. Most of the rest of Snape and Dumbledore's relationship, fascinating though it is, plays out on screen in "The Prince's Tale," and we will return to it in due course.

The Winky Question

There is one question about Dumbledore that seems so obvious, I never thought to ask it until my fifteenth reread of the series. When Dumbledore rescues Harry from the clutches of Fake Moody after Harry returns from the graveyard, he issues a host of instructions to McGonagall and Snape before he actually begins questioning Crouch Jr. Why does Dumbledore tell Snape to fetch Winky before the Polyjuice wears off of the imposter Moody?

The obvious answer is that he knew it was Crouch Jr. masquerading as Moody, which is why I never thought twice about it. But how could he know? What is the logical leap from "There is someone Polyjuiced as Moody" to "Barty Crouch Jr. is the culprit"?

Kearns credits the "Madness of Mr. Crouch" episode with tipping Dumbledore off, but this is the main point on which I disagree with her essay. The only thing Harry says to Dumbledore is, "[Mr. Crouch] Said he wants to warn you... said he's done something terrible... he mentioned his son... and Bertha Jorkins ... and—and Voldemort... something about Voldemort getting stronger...." (GF558)

Trying to look at it from the outsider's perspective, the bit about his son seems to be the least significant portion of this sentence. He's done something terrible in connection to Bertha Jorkins, whose disappearance Dumbledore already assumed was linked to Voldemort getting stronger... what could the "something terrible" be? Mentioning his son, alongside mentions of Percy Weasley, could very well be part of his raving, or a late-onset guilt trip, as Hermione points out. There's a missing step in the logical leap from this to Crouch Jr. being alive and the culprit.

Dumbledore has not yet put it all together, as evidenced by what we see in the Pensieve—the closest we ever get to seeing Dumbledore's mind at work. If Dumbledore knew Crouch Jr. was the suspect at this point, why would he be reviewing the trials of Karkaroff and Bagman? He already knows they're acting shifty, but what could he hope to glean about Crouch Jr. from reliving their trials?

Dumbledore's choice of memories to peruse is highly significant. He is looking for people who have grudges against Crouch Sr. (because it's obvious there is now foul play at work). First on the list would be Death Eaters he put on trial. His chief suspects are Karkaroff and Bagman, but neither seems like the guy. Dumbledore may be intrigued enough about the mention of Crouch's son to view the trial of Barty Crouch Jr., or he may just be doing a thorough job, but if he knew Junior was the culprit, he'd have no reason to watch the other trials. He is also still trying to figure out how Bertha and Crouch Sr. are connected, since he is examining memories of her.

Dumbledore is also unsure about another key piece of information: whether Crouch Jr. even was a Death Eater. Prior to Crouch Jr.'s boastful confession under the influence of Veritaserum, no one really knew whether he was a Death Eater or whether he had "been in the wrong place at the wrong time." (GF528) Sirius has "no idea" whether Crouch Jr. is a Death Eater (GF528).

When Crouch Jr. was captured, he "can't have been more than nineteen," (GF528) so he would have been a fairly new recruit, without much of a Death Eater reputation. Crouch Jr. certainly put on a convincing performance of innocence during his trial. Voldemort made sure the Death Eaters didn't know each other, so no Death Eater can provide negative confirmation of Crouch Jr. being one of them. In any event, when Dumbledore is puzzling this out, he is not on speaking terms with the one Death Eater he could ordinarily ask about these things: Snape. All this combines to make Dumbledore unsure whether Crouch Jr. even is a Death Eater, so it would be a huge leap from that to "Junior faked his death and is the evil mastermind at work."

A possibility that we should not discount is that this is as far as Dumbledore ever got in figuring it out. In this scenario, Dumbledore did not know about Crouch Jr. until the moment the Polyjuice wore off, and he called for Winky because he knew the Crouch family would be somehow involved. It's a plausible alternative to what I believe actually happened, so it bears mentioning.

However, assuming Dumbledore is as resourceful and determined as we know him to be, there is still one avenue of inquiry he can pursue to find out what was going on with Mr. Crouch. Even if that would not tie in to whatever else was going on, once Dumbledore knew something was very fishy with Crouch Sr. (and had exhausted all other lines of inquiry like watching Pensieve memories), Dumbledore would have gone to Winky and used Legilimency on her. This is likely because we know of at least one other instance when Dumbledore used Legilimency on a house-elf to get crucial information: Kreacher at the end of Book 5 (OP832).

So if this happened, what would Dumbledore glean from this? He would know nothing about Crouch Jr. impersonating Moody or working for Voldemort, because Winky was fired before that happened. At most, this would tell Dumbledore that Crouch Jr. was still alive. He would also learn of the Quidditch World Cup episode and of how Bertha's memory was damaged. But none of these things answer any of the questions that Dumbledore needs answered: who put Harry's name in the Goblet, and how, and why.

If one reads Dumbledore's interrogation of Crouch Jr. under Veritaserum assuming he knows all that Winky's mind had to offer, parts of it seem superfluous. Dumbledore could have expedited the questioning about Barty's faked death and the World Cup episode if he knew it all already. However, Dumbledore is going through the whole story more for Harry's benefit than for his own and is being thorough for that purpose. (And if I may break the fourth wall, we should also consider that Rowling is going through it for the readers' benefit.)

I think it probable that Dumbledore did read Winky's mind to glean all she knew, otherwise he just wasn't as thorough as we've come to expect from him. And he is definitely curious about what Crouch Jr. is up to now that his father's gone crazy and disappeared. But it would then take quite an impressive logical leap to assume that Crouch Jr. is the mystery Death Eater involved in Voldemort's scheme. If anyone is capable of making that leap, it's Dumbledore... but it's more likely that until the very last moment, Crouch Jr. is just an additional suspect on the list alongside Bagman and Karkaroff.

When Fake Moody whisks Harry away after the third task, Dumbledore's mind begins whirring. It's time to use process of elimination! He's reasonably confident that the real Moody can throw off the Imperius Curse, especially after a year, so it has to be

Polyjuice Potion at work. Both Bagman and Karkaroff have been present at the same time as Moody (right after Harry's name came out of the Goblet of Fire, for example). So if it isn't either of them, it has to be another Death Eater—all of the ones presumed alive have been accounted for at some point during the year. Wormtail can be ruled out by Harry's dream (GF599). That leaves three options, however far-fetched, for the mystery Death Eater:

- Crouch Jr.—Still a definite possibility.
- Bertha Jorkins under the Imperius Curse—Dumbledore does not know that she is dead, as Harry only tells him that Crouch Sr. mentioned her. However, pulling off this kind of ruse for a year while under the Imperius Curse would be stretching the boundaries of plausibility.
- Yet another Death Eater returned from the dead—Dumbledore has now discovered that two Death Eaters thought dead are very much alive, all in the span of a year; he has to be wondering if there are yet more out there.

Of the three options, the simplest and likeliest one is Crouch Jr. Dumbledore tends to trust his guesses, because his "guesses have usually been good." (DH710) And that is how, at the very last possible moment, Dumbledore figures out that Crouch Jr. is masquerading as Moody and calls for Winky to be present at his unmasking. It's a testament to both Crouch Jr.'s skills and Voldemort's scheming that it took Dumbledore this long.

Lord Voldemort's Propaganda

There's a reason I'm writing a book about Dumbledore's modus operandi when it comes to plotting against Voldemort, and not the other way around. Between Voldemort's Evil Overlord Syndrome making him constantly expound upon his evil plots, and Dumbledore's propensity to psychoanalyze Voldemort, we have a very good idea of how Voldemort's mind works. In addition, Voldemort's plots are usually very straightforward compared to Dumbledore's. He wants something (the Sorcerer's Stone, the prophecy, Dumbledore's death), so he gets someone to go after it for him (Quirrell, Harry, Draco and Snape) through a mixture of coercion and deceit.

Now that Voldemort is back, Dumbledore's plans will depend a lot on what he does. To fully understand Dumbledore, we must briefly examine how Voldemort operates. And this proves to be the antithesis of how Dumbledore operates. Voldemort is constantly proclaiming to everyone how awesome his plans are, how all-powerful and clever he is, and how Harry Potter does not stand a chance against him. Everyone always knows what his plans are and what he'll do.

Contrast this with Dumbledore, whose plans no one knows. Dumbledore does not seek recognition for his triumphs, he commands respect without demanding it—Dobby is allowed to call him "a barmy old codger." (GF380) In fact, no one but Harry, Ron, and Hermione even knows the extent of what Dumbledore has done to combat Voldemort. This is why I have spent years unraveling Dumbledore's plans: one of their main features is that no one knows what they are. That is why, with the exception of the events of *Goblet of Fire*, he manages to stay two steps ahead of Voldemort. Voldemort, through his theatrics, becomes predictable; Dumbledore remains unknowable.

However, in *Goblet of Fire*, Dumbledore fails to stay ahead of Voldemort. So I would like to zero in on Voldemort's most elaborate scheme: the year-long plot in *Goblet of Fire* that culminated in his resurrection. This is the first and last time that Voldemort is executing his plans with Dumbledore being none the wiser. As Hagrid says, "Worried! I dunno when I seen Dumbledore more worried than he's bin lately." (GF563)

Why is it this plan that tripped up Dumbledore? I believe it's for the same reason readers so often roll their eyes at *Goblet of Fire*: from a logical standpoint, Voldemort's plan seems ludicrous. To recap Voldemort's plan:

- Have Barty Crouch Jr. pretend to be Alastor Moody at Hogwarts, right under Dumbledore's nose. Have him keep this up for an entire year, teaching the children and everything.
- Imposter Moody will manage to Confund the Goblet of Fire into accepting Harry Potter as a Triwizard Champion.
- Imposter Moody will surreptitiously assist Harry in the Tournament, getting a fourteen-year-old through tasks that challenge the most prodigious seventeen-year-olds, while ensuring Crouch's hand in it cannot be seen.

After all that, after a year as a Hogwarts professor and the entire Triwizard Tournament, Imposter Moody will transform the Triwizard Cup into a Portkey to spirit Harry away from Hogwarts, setting the stage for Voldemort's resurrection.

This all begs the question: why not have Imposter Moody give Harry a Portkey on the first day of classes in the form of a textbook or something, and bypass all the tournament shenanigans altogether?

A brief aside about Portkeys:

The mechanics of Portkeys are rather confusing, based on some conflicting evidence that stemmed from plot necessity. As near as I can figure, anyone can make Portkeys out of Hogwarts, but only Dumbledore—or the current headmaster at any given point—can create Portkeys into Hogwarts. This checks out with Dumbledore creating a Portkey for Harry at the end of *Order of the Phoenix* and does not contradict all the magical protections surrounding Hogwarts. After all, that would be a pretty big gaping hole in Hogwarts's defenses if anyone could Portkey in.

This leads to the conclusion that the Triwizard Cup was made into a Portkey by Dumbledore to take whoever touched it back onto Hogwarts grounds. That's further supported by the logistics of the Third Task, since any other way for the champions to emerge from the maze would feel distinctly anticlimactic. When Crouch Jr. says he "turned it into a Portkey," (GF691), that's probably shorthand for adding an intermediate stop to the existing Portkey. The Portkey was always going to go back to Hogwarts grounds, but Crouch made sure that first it went to the graveyard and Voldemort. This explains why the Cup returned Harry to Hogwarts, since no one seemed surprised by him Portkeying in. But this reinforces the idea that Fake Moody could have Portkeyed Harry away at any time; the tricky part would have been getting him back.

So, the main question: why a plot that is so needlessly elaborate, where so much can (and nearly does) go wrong?

Because Voldemort fears Dumbledore. Lupin says, "the very last person [Voldemort] wanted alerted to his return the moment he got back was Dumbledore," (OP92) and I think that is the answer to all of this. If Harry suddenly disappears one night, Dumbledore will immediately suspect Voldemort's involvement, and will use all of his considerable resources and ingenuity to find out what's going on. Then Voldemort, with no more than a score of Death Eaters, will have Dumbledore after him.

However, if Harry disappears during the Third Triwizard Task, it can be disguised as an unfortunate accident. That is why the Triwizard Cup was left a Portkey twice over: once to bring Harry to Voldemort, a second time to send him back to Hogwarts. Crouch Jr. intended for Harry's corpse to return to Hogwarts after Voldemort killed him.

Note that no one can see what's happening inside the maze. But everyone knows there are lots of deadly things in there (acromantulas, sphinxes, etc.). So assume Harry's dead body and the Triwizard Cup arrive on the Hogwarts grounds. The immediate conclusion would be that he was mauled to death by a sphinx or something, managing to grab the Cup at the very last second. For added effect, Voldemort can have Nagini bite Harry's corpse to give the illusion of death by magical creature. To be sure, Dumbledore would be suspicious, but he wouldn't know for certain that Voldemort was responsible. Then Voldemort can run amok in the world, recruiting and wreaking havoc while no one is the wiser.

It was just Voldemort's bad luck that neither of the first two tasks was conducive to such a ruse. The first task, the dragons, was done in full view of everyone, so Harry could not be spirited away unobtrusively. The second task was unseen by spectators, but there was nothing in the lake that would actually kill Harry. If his dead body floated to the surface, there will have been no question of foul play. But the third task was perfect—invisible and deadly, so Voldemort had to bide his time until June.

Why didn't Dumbledore pick up on this? I think because he did not realize how much of a priority secrecy was to Voldemort. Voldemort is a master of publicity and propaganda, because he realizes how effective those tools are. He fashioned himself a new name, then made the entire world afraid to speak it. He created a logo, the Dark Mark, that he burned into his followers' skin, and that he cast into the sky to signify murder. "Just picture coming home and finding the Dark Mark hovering over your house, and knowing what you're about to find inside...." Mr. Weasley winced. "Everyone's worst fear... the very worst..." (GF142) This is the kind of branding that most companies would kill for. So Dumbledore does not realize how badly Voldemort wants to preserve his anonymity here, and therefore can't figure out what Voldemort's planning.

It's also worth noting that, contrary to all precedent, Voldemort actually wants Harry alive for his revival potion. Considering all the energy expounded to kill Harry in previous years, this further trips up Dumbledore.

Give Voldemort this: he is an absolute master of theatricality. It is one of his most important tools in maintaining control of the Death Eaters. And it also serves to foil his plans time and time again. Voldemort hits every Evil Overlord cliché head-on: he loves to hear himself talk, and he always plays with his food, to his detriment.[32]

While there is much to recommend using Harry Potter for his resurrection, I believe that Voldemort's primary purpose was to make a point to the Death Eaters. At the end of *Goblet of Fire*, Voldemort is essentially giving a show to the Death Eaters; he stops just short of a big musical number. He uses Harry's blood to show that if there is anything special about Harry, Voldemort now has it. He drones extensively about his awesome evil plots, showing off how he pulled off such a cool thing right under Dumbledore's nose. And then, to show the Death Eaters once and for all who's boss, he lets Harry attempt to duel him. He tortures Harry, forces Harry to bow to him, and does everything in his power to prove to the Death Eaters how powerless Harry is against him. This is all smart image control by Voldemort, up until the part where Harry gets away thanks to an unforeseen Priori Incantatem.

However, give Voldemort this: his plan in *Goblet of Fire* is a masterstroke. He deals with two issues at once: regaining the Death Eaters' respect and leaving Dumbledore none the wiser. While he rather fails at the second point, it is due to "luck and chance, those wreckers of all but the best-laid plans." (DH7) But imagine, if you will, that Priori Incantatem had not occurred. The Death Eaters are in awe of Voldemort, Dumbledore and the Ministry know nothing and let Voldemort run amok. When Voldemort does finally

---

[32] He is most guilty of this in *Chamber of Secrets*, when he was putting on a show without even having an audience there. But that can be attributed to the arrogance of youth—if the adult Voldemort is full of himself, it's nothing compared to the self-satisfied teenage version. And the habit of wanting to win in style is a hard one to break.

come out into the open, there is no Harry Potter to be a figurehead for the rebellion.

We will see how much Voldemort values his anonymity in the Ministry's eyes based on his behavior in *Order of the Phoenix*. Because although Harry manages to warn Dumbledore in time, Voldemort is aided in keeping his cover by a rather odd pair of people: an unscrupulous journalist and a career politician who loves his job too much. And this will leave Dumbledore fighting battles on multiple fronts for the next year.

Chapter 5:
Albus Dumbledore and the Order of the Phoenix

The Sluggish Memory

Before we get into what Dumbledore was doing in *Order of the Phoenix*, it's necessary to take stock of what he actually knew at this juncture in the series. Let us first revisit the question of what Dumbledore knew about Horcruxes at this point. If you'll recall, Dumbledore had his first breakthrough at the end of *Chamber of Secrets*, where the weaponization of the diary indicated that Voldemort might have made more than one Horcrux. But as we've discussed, Dumbledore had a rather hectic two years since then, and even if he started doing his research into Tom Riddle's history, it was not at the top of his priority list. However, at the end of *Goblet of Fire*, there is another breakthrough, and this one's a game-changer.

As Harry is once again relating his adventures in Dumbledore's office, he reports that Lord Voldemort has risen again and that Voldemort gave a very insightful monologue to his Death Eaters. Dumbledore later tells Harry his thought process at the moment.

> "[Voldemort] made a most illuminating and alarming statement to his Death Eaters. 'I, who have gone further than anybody along the path that leads to immortality.' That was what you told me he said. 'Further than anybody.' And I

> thought I knew what that meant, though the Death Eaters did not. He was referring to his Horcruxes, Horcruxes in the plural, Harry, which I do not believe any other wizard has ever had. Yet it fitted: Lord Voldemort has seemed to grow less human with the passing years, and the transformation he has undergone seemed to me to be only explicable if his soul was mutilated beyond the realms of what we might call 'usual evil' . . ." (HBP501-2)

An interesting point to consider is that this passage seems to indicate that Dumbledore used Legilimency on Harry as Harry related the events in the graveyard. It is wholly implausible that a severely traumatized Harry would be able to recite Voldemort's speech word-for-word after the night he'd just had—after all, he's not Hermione! It's curious to consider how many times Dumbledore performed Legilimency on Harry over the years, but we now have two instances that are almost certain.

Anyway, now Dumbledore's two-year-old theory is confirmed: that Voldemort did indeed make multiple Horcruxes. And now Dumbledore has to do research! What are the other Horcruxes? Dumbledore already has some solid candidates for what might be a Horcrux—Slytherin's locket, the Peverell ring, and Hufflepuff's Cup.[33] With the diary, that's already four.

---

[33] I base this on the assumption that Dumbledore has already viewed Morfin and Hokey's memories by the beginning of Book 5. We cannot be certain of this, but Dumbledore says that he "attempted to use [the memory] to secure Morfin's release from Azkaban." (HBP368) This would have been a fool's errand after Dumbledore and Fudge's parting of ways, so it probably happened before that.

But Dumbledore has one huge unanswered question here: how many Horcruxes are there total? Would Voldemort have dared to make four Horcruxes? Or did he make even more than that? This is the most important piece of information that Dumbledore needs. After all, wouldn't it be awful if Dumbledore destroyed ten Horcruxes and attempted to kill Voldemort, only to find out that Voldemort had made an even dozen? Or inversely, what if Dumbledore wasted time hunting for a sixth and seventh Horcrux if Voldemort only made five, and innocent people died in the meantime? Dumbledore needed to know exactly how many Horcruxes there were! And in the meantime, he could start researching what and where the Horcruxes might be.

Of course, this is all easier said than done. How could he find out how many Horcruxes Voldemort made? Short of asking Voldemort himself, there seems to be no possible way. Unless... what if, when Tom Riddle was learning about Horcruxes, he decided on a certain number? Eventually, this line of thinking would lead Dumbledore straight to Slughorn.

I believe Dumbledore got the altered memory from Slughorn that very summer in 1995. Upon seeing that Slughorn had made it useless by excluding the only information Dumbledore needed—the planned number of Horcruxes—Dumbledore attempted to lure Slughorn to a job at Hogwarts.

Didn't it ever strike anyone as odd that Dumbledore was completely unable to find a D.A.D.A. professor in 1995? Sure, the applicant pool is rather thin after a four-decade-long curse. But we've seen that Dumbledore has no objection to hiring substandard professors when he needs them there (see: Hagrid, Trelawney, etc.). And keeping Umbridge out of Hogwarts would seem like a pretty big priority, so why wouldn't Dumbledore just ask Kingsley or someone to fill in for a year?

Because Dumbledore was keeping a position open for Slughorn, that's why. He wanted Slughorn to come back to Hogwarts, where Dumbledore could work on extracting that much-needed memory from him. And then Snape would be put in the D.A.D.A. position, because Snape is still needed at Hogwarts as well. Dumbledore was so desperate to get Slughorn that he did not even make a back-up plan, which is how Umbridge got foisted onto Hogwarts at the very last second.

The Scar

When Dumbledore received confirmation of his theory about Horcruxes, this allowed him to make another important deduction: the likelihood of Harry's scar containing a bit of Voldemort's soul. When I first wrote about Dumbledore and Horcruxes, many of my readers took issue with the theory that Dumbledore did not know everything about the Scarcrux prior to *Order of the Phoenix*, based on the conversation he had with Harry at the end of *Chamber of Secrets*.

> "Unless I'm much mistaken, he transferred some of his own powers to you the night he gave you that scar. Not something he intended to do, I'm sure..."
>
> "Voldemort put a bit of himself in me?" Harry said, thunderstruck.
>
> "It certainly seems so." (CS333)

The interpretation here hinges on whether Dumbledore means "a bit of himself" literally—I believe he does not. He merely refers to the transfer of powers as a bit of Voldemort, instead of referring to a bit of soul. We must keep in mind that Harry and Voldemort are delving into unknown realms of magic. Dumbledore did not even know that Voldemort had split his soul until the end of *Chamber of Secrets*. He would not have made the leap that Voldemort's soul was so unstable as to have bits flying off it, not until he received confirmation at the end of *Goblet of Fire* about Voldemort's multiple Horcruxes. We are not privy to Dumbledore's vast knowledge of obscure magic, so there may well have been another possibility for Harry receiving Voldemort's powers through the curse.

This helps exonerate Dumbledore from the charge Snape levelled at him, of raising Harry like a pig for slaughter. Up until Harry was fifteen, Dumbledore did not know that Harry would need to die. He was only keeping the prophecy from Harry, not the knowledge that Harry may have to sacrifice himself. Dumbledore was raising Harry to be a Voldemort slayer—the morality of that can still be debated, but it's not quite as morally repugnant.

Note that even Voldemort, the one who actually made Horcruxes and is probably the world's leading expert on them, did not realize that Harry's scar had bits of soul in it. Voldemort didn't realize this even after he found out about the mental connection he shared with Harry. If Voldemort didn't come to the realization, with all the knowledge he's privy to, it's small wonder that it took Dumbledore a while.

Another slight point in favor of Dumbledore not knowing is a line from the very first chapter of the series, when McGonagall asks if he can do something about baby Harry's scar: "Even if I could, I wouldn't. Scars can come in handy." (SS15) I believe Dumbledore truly did not suspect Harry's scar of containing

Voldemort's soul, or he would not have been so glib about it—this is a case of irony coming from the author, not from Dumbledore himself.

Towards the end of *Goblet of Fire*, we see that Dumbledore is closer to figuring it all out. He says, "I have a theory, no more than that.... It is my belief that your scar hurts both when Lord Voldemort is near you, and when he is feeling a particularly strong surge of hatred. [...] Because you and he are connected by the curse that failed. [...] That is no ordinary scar." (GF600)

The problem is that because Dumbledore is always deliberately keeping this information from Harry, the language used intentionally obfuscates whether Dumbledore knew about the Scarcrux. Dumbledore only ever refers to a "connection:" in the *Order of the Phoenix* tell-all, he says, "I guessed, fifteen years ago, when I saw the scar upon your forehead, what it might mean. I guessed that it might be the sign of a connection forged between you and Voldemort." (OP826-827)

We don't know whether "connected" is Dumbledore-speak for "swapped soul bits," but either way Dumbledore is still uncertain about whether Harry's scar is an unintentional Horcrux in *Goblet of Fire*. He may have his theories and guesses, but is not confident in said theory until Harry brings back confirmation that Voldemort was indeed splitting his soul multiple times. And even then, though Dumbledore formulated a theory about the Scarcrux by the beginning of OotP, he is still piecing it together through the end of 1995, unable to get confirmation and obstructed by Harry's reluctance to actually discuss his scar hurting.

So as all this is going on, Dumbledore comes to an important realization: he needs to buy some time. And he has a pretty shrewd idea of how to do so.

Dumbledore's Decoy

As will often come up in a discussion of the books, *Order of the Phoenix* was always my least favorite of the seven books. Not for any of the usual reasons: I never had issues with Harry's fondness for CapsLock or Sirius dying. Rather, it's because the entire book seemed rather pointless. All the other books move the story along as a whole, but what does OotP accomplish? After 800-odd pages, we have learned that... (drumroll, please!) Harry and Voldemort will have to kill each other! Gee, who saw that coming?

After all the hype and hoopla, we found out what should have been obvious from the first book: that the hero will defeat the villain. In vain, readers tried to find meaning in the prophecy, and flooded the HP fansites with essays in 2003 and 2004. Instead of all the Horcruxes debate, the fandom spent two years analyzing the prophecy. It was taken apart, every word analyzed and every ellipsis examined, as people looked for loopholes and alternate meanings.[34]

But we now have the gift of hindsight and know that there really was no dramatic revelation to be found in the prophecy. This holds true even if we build up that fourth wall again and look at it from the point

---

[34] There were a lot of questions that assiduous fans sought answers to: Would Harry live or die? Would Tom Riddle die along with Voldemort? Would Neville's status as an also-ran Chosen One factor in at all?
As the debate raged on, the interpretations became more and more creative, like the one stating that Harry would have to rapidly conceive another child to be born at the end of July, and *that* kid would be the one to finish off Voldemort. (It was a compelling theory, based on the repetition of the line "the one with the power to vanquish the Dark Lord will be born as the seventh month dies..." In one fanfiction I read, Hermione delivered a magical PowerPoint presentation to Harry and Dumbledore all about it.)

of view of the characters. Yes, it's important and significant to Harry... but it really should not matter that much to anyone else in the wizarding world. After all, there's nothing really to be gleaned from it. So why all the fuss?

Well, that question is answered rather easily: the prophecy is a decoy. It serves to keep Voldemort busy. It's Dumbledore at work, being five steps ahead of everyone else. Just like in *Sorcerer's Stone*, Dumbledore likes keeping Voldemort busy and knowing what he's up to, so he dangles a carrot in front of Voldemort's nonexistent nose for the better part of a year.

Let's look at Dumbledore's point of view at the end of *Goblet of Fire*. Voldemort has just returned to power. And because Dumbledore knows Voldemort, Dumbledore can guess what's on Voldemort's long-term agenda.

Lord Voldemort's Evil To-Do List, June 1995

1. Kill Harry Potter. (But do it in style.)
2. Kill Albus Dumbledore. With Dumbledore gone, no one will be able to oppose me. This will also make achieving point #1 much easier.
3. Spring Death Eaters from Azkaban. Need more loyal and intelligent supporters. This will help to achieve point #2. Not to mention, Bellatrix Lestrange is easy on the eyes.
4. Take over Ministry of Magic. Those fools are ignoring my return, which will make killing/Imperiusing them very easy. I will now be supreme ruler of the wizarding Britain! Muahahahaha!!
5. Start Mudblood genocide.
6. Live evilly ever after.

We know this based on what Voldemort ends up doing in the latter books, but Dumbledore is shrewd enough to figure it out long before the reader. Stopping all these plots would take far too much energy, and Dumbledore is also a touch rattled by how successful Voldemort's plot the prior year turned out to be. Better get a head start on bringing down Voldemort, so Dumbledore needs to find something relatively innocuous to occupy Voldemort while Dumbledore begins working on his own plans. And then Dumbledore is visited by one of his more brilliant ideas: since Harry escaped Voldemort, Voldemort will be obsessing over how to kill this boy once and for all. Voldemort will try to glean information from the prophecy. Dumbledore says as much during his "tell-all" conversation with Harry at the end of OotP:

> "And so, since his return to his body, and particularly since your extraordinary escape from him last year, he has been determined to hear that prophecy in its entirety. This is the weapon he has been seeking so assiduously since his return: the knowledge of how to destroy you." (OP739-740)

So why not keep him chasing after the prophecy while Dumbledore starts taking productive measures to stop him? It's easier for Dumbledore to do his thing without Voldemort breathing down his neck. Lucky for Dumbledore, the prophecy would be useless to Voldemort, so it's okay to send him on a wild goose chase for it.[35]

---

[35] Dumbledore probably told Snape to subtly encourage this quest of Voldemort's—the usefulness of double agents!

Let's look at what the prophecy actually says:

> "The one with the power to vanquish the Dark Lord approaches... born to those who have thrice defied him, born as the seventh month dies... and the Dark Lord will mark him as his equal, but he will have power the Dark Lord knows not... and either must die at the hand of the other for neither can live while the other survives... the one with the power to vanquish the Dark Lord will be born as the seventh month dies..." (OP841)

First, keep in mind that Voldemort already knows almost half the prophecy because Snape overheard it. According to Dumbledore, "He heard only the beginning, the part foretelling the birth of a boy in July to parents who had thrice defied Voldemort." (OP743)

Of the information that's left, there are two salient points. The first is that "the Dark Lord will mark him as his equal, but he will have power the Dark Lord knows not." But this is all in the past already, and Voldemort already suspects Harry has some power that he does not because the boy keeps not dying and keeps stymying his evil plots. This information would be no help to Voldemort.

The second point is that "either must die at the hand of the other." Well, Voldemort certainly intends to kill Harry, so that information does not really help him either. In short, there is no information that Voldemort can glean from this prophecy that would merit so much fuss being made about it.

What's more, after two years of the fandom agonizing over this prophecy, and several months of Harry worrying about it, Dumbledore comes right out and says that it doesn't matter! During one of his private lessons with Harry in *Half-Blood Prince*, Dumbledore gets very agitated, and finally tells Harry, "You are setting too much store by the prophecy!" (HBP509)

Even Harry feels the anticlimax of all this. "'So, when the prophecy says that I'll have "power the Dark Lord knows not," it just means—love?' asked Harry, feeling a little let down." (HBP509)

Harry believes that the prophecy requires him to kill Voldemort, but Dumbledore disagrees, and moreover exclaims that, "It is essential that you understand this!" (HBP510) Dumbledore then explains to us, conclusively, that the prophecy does not matter at all.

> "Imagine, please, just for a moment, that you had never heard that prophecy! How would you feel about Voldemort now? Think!"
>
> [...]
>
> "I'd want him finished," said Harry quietly. "And I'd want to do it."
>
> "Of course you would!" cried Dumbledore. "You see, the prophecy does not mean you have to do anything! But the prophecy caused Lord Voldemort to mark you as his equal... in other words, you are free to choose your way, quite free to turn your back on the prophecy! But Voldemort continues to set store by the prophecy. He will continue to hunt you... which makes it certain, really, that—"
>
> "That one of us is going to end up killing the other," said Harry. "Yes." (HBP511-512)

And there you have it. The prophecy's only importance in the story is the backstory it provides on why Voldemort initially attacked Harry and set this entire chain of events in motion. At this point, Harry and Voldemort will fight to the death regardless of the prophecy, and Dumbledore is well aware of this.

So the obvious conclusion is that Dumbledore used the prophecy as a decoy to keep Voldemort busy during his first year back. But what's astonishing is how far this deception went and how Machiavellian Dumbledore was about the whole thing. Indeed, thus far it can be argued that Dumbledore's actions have all been unequivocally good, but now we enter the phase of some murkier morality in his actions.

The Order's Role

Dumbledore funnels most of his considerable resources into keeping Voldemort away from the prophecy. Considering what is being guarded, this appears totally unwarranted—but if the prophecy is a decoy, then it would be a top priority to keep it from Voldemort.

One of the Order's main tasks is the guard duty over this object. Logistically, this is impressive: Dumbledore puts in the effort to sneak people into the Ministry undetected to keep a 24/7 watch on this prophecy. And considering the entire Order of the Phoenix seems to be roughly twenty people, that is a considerable portion of their finite resources being used to guard this prophecy and keep Voldemort at bay.

But here is the scary part: the Order does not actually know that they are guarding a decoy. They seem convinced that keeping Voldemort from this prophecy is a matter of life and death, not just a stalling technique. After Mr. Weasley is attacked by Nagini, Sirius says, "there are things worth dying for!"

(OP477) He is evidently convinced that protecting this prophecy is one of those worthy things. Dumbledore does nothing to disabuse the Order of this notion, not even when Sturgis Podmore is carted off to Azkaban or Mr. Weasley gets almost fatally attacked by Nagini while on guard duty.

And digging deeper, it becomes evident that the Order does not even know what it is they are guarding!

> [Sirius said,] "In any case, gathering followers is only one thing [Voldemort]'s interested in. He's got other plans too, plans he can put into operation very quietly indeed, and he's concentrating on those for the moment."
>
> "What's he after apart from followers?" Harry asked swiftly. He thought he saw Sirius and Lupin exchange the most fleeting of looks before Sirius answered.
>
> "Stuff he can only get by stealth."
>
> When Harry continued to look puzzled, Sirius said, "Like a weapon. Something he didn't have last time." (OP96)

This passage is Jo at her finest—misdirection galore! She makes it appear as if the Order knows all there is to know. But if one looks at the information given, it seems like the only thing the Order knows is that they are guarding something in the Department of Mysteries... and that this is Voldemort's focus at the moment.

For years, this passage bothered me. Why on earth does Sirius refer to the prophecy as a "weapon?" This term is emphasized quite a bit throughout the rest of the book as a red herring for us and for Harry. But

Sirius is always direct with Harry and would not intentionally deceive him. And I doubt he would view it as Dumbledore did, where the "weapon" is the knowledge of how to destroy Harry.

The only logical conclusion is that Sirius—and, by extension, the Order—truly believes that they are guarding a dangerous weapon from Voldemort. And this is just blatantly untrue. But it's also classic Dumbledore.

Aberforth says of his brother, "Secrets and lies, that's how we grew up, and Albus . . . he was a natural." (DH562) Dumbledore never trusted anyone completely and kept all his cards extremely close to his chest, particularly after Voldemort was reborn. He would not trust the Order with the information that they were a mere distraction for Voldemort. Rather, he allowed them to believe that they were doing something worth risking their lives for, thereby ensuring the ruse was complete. And he was willing to let members nearly die just to keep Voldemort occupied a little longer.

A Livejournal user, Sophierom, wrote that a central theme in *Order of the Phoenix* is that hierarchical relationships are bad, whereas relationships built on commonality and equality are good.[36] This is an important lens through which to view Dumbledore's actions here: Dumbledore's relationship with the other members of the Order is not equal, and his deception of them is an abuse of power. This is in sharp contrast to Dumbledore's Army, where the leader is a fellow student, and is even democratically chosen (OP391).

Considering the very high price Dumbledore was willing to pay, one just hopes that whatever he was taking this time to do was worth it. . .

---

[36] "Dumbledore's Decisions and the Vulnerability of Authority." https://hp-essays.livejournal.com/62338.html

In Essence Divided

With the time that the decoy bought him, Dumbledore digs deep into Tom Riddle's past. This time period, the latter half of 1995, is when Dumbledore did his most intense research. He is still missing the crucial number of Horcruxes, but Dumbledore is not sitting idly by while he figures that out. No, he is reviewing memories of Tom Riddle to figure out what the Horcruxes might be.

When he has lessons with Harry in HBP, the memories have been carefully curated to display the Horcruxes. But that's just the tip of the iceberg—Dumbledore did not get Tom Riddle's past pre-packaged into a half-dozen memories that perfectly display relevant information. He had to peruse all possible data about Tom Riddle—and first, all those memories (useful or useless) had to be obtained, sometimes with great difficulty. He must have looked through dozens or hundreds of memories, including his own, of Riddle's seven years at Hogwarts, keeping an eye out for potential Horcruxes and their possible hiding places. He must have found myriad false clues as he worked on connecting the dots. This would have taken him most of Harry's fifth year at Hogwarts.

It's no wonder Dumbledore seems stressed out in *Order of the Phoenix*—he's fighting three battles at once! He has the Order pitted against Voldemort and the Death Eaters to keep everyone busy with the prophecy, he is battling Umbridge and Fudge's meddling at Hogwarts, and he is attempting to research the Horcruxes.

By the end of 1995, Dumbledore has perused the memories enough to be reasonably confident in the locket, ring, and cup as Horcruxes. He is developing a rather sinister theory about Harry's scar being an unintentional Horcrux. (This is a separate line of questioning for Dumbledore, since Harry was obviously not intended to be a Horcrux among Voldemort's fixed set.) And he also begins to have some niggling suspicions about a less conventional Horcrux candidate: Voldemort's snake Nagini seems to be strangely obedient to Voldemort, even given that he's a Parselmouth. Hmm...

Suddenly one night, Harry is in Dumbledore's office again, saying he had ventured into Voldemort's mind while Voldemort was in Nagini's mind. Dumbledore taps one of his instruments, which emits a smoky snake. Dumbledore asks, "But in essence divided?" and the snake splits in two, which confirms whatever Dumbledore is thinking (OP470).

This tiny passage caused more speculation than almost any other in the first six books.[37] Finally, after *Deathly Hallows* was released, Jo told us what it meant in an interview.

"Dumbledore suspected that the snake's essence was divided—that it contained part of Voldemort's soul, and that was why it was so very adept at doing his bidding. This also explained why Harry, the last and unintended Horcrux, could see so clearly though the snake's eyes, just as he regularly sees through Voldemort's. Dumbledore is thinking aloud here, edging towards the truth with the help of the Pensieve." [38]

So there, in one fell swoop, Dumbledore confirms his suspicions about two Horcruxes: Nagini and the unintentional Horcrux in Harry's scar. Upon confirming the exact nature of Harry's connection to Voldemort and realizing that Voldemort is now aware of the mental

---

[37] Rivaled only by Dumbledore's "gleam of triumph" and the prophecy itself, if my memory serves.
[38] From the JK Rowling web chat hosted by Bloomsbury, July 31, 2007, http://www.accio-quote.org/articles/2007/0730-bloomsbury-chat.html.

aspect of the connection, Dumbledore wastes no time in setting up Harry's Occlumency lessons.

Dumbledore cannot do anything about Nagini the Horcrux just yet, and certainly nothing about Harry. And he still does not know how many Horcruxes were created. However, he knows it would be sensible of Voldemort to have at least one traditional Horcrux designed only to keep the piece of soul safe, and neither the diary nor Nagini qualify because they are both intended for offensive use.

Nagini is frequently sent forth to do Voldemort's bidding, like sneaking into the Ministry of Magic or biting Hogwarts faculty. As for the diary, "Riddle really wanted that diary read, wanted the piece of his soul to inhabit or possess somebody else, so that Slytherin's monster would be unleashed again." (HBP501) With both of these, Voldemort used the bits of his soul as weapons in his arsenal, but that lessened their effectiveness as safeguards of his immortality. As Dumbledore tells Harry, "The point of a Horcrux is [. . .] to keep part of the self hidden and safe, not to fling it into somebody else's path and run the risk that they might destroy it—as indeed happened." (HBP501) So there is at least one other Horcrux out there that Voldemort is using defensively, as it was intended.

Of the other potential candidates, Dumbledore is fairly confident that the Peverell ring is one, since he has Morfin's memory and likely saw Tom Riddle wearing it. Something should be done about that, but Dumbledore's moves are limited for the next four months. . . until a certain sneak helps him out without realizing it.

Hunting Horcruxes

At first glance, the Horcrux hunt only began in *Half-Blood Prince*, which should strike the attentive reader as rather odd. After all, why wait to start hunting them down? Well, actually, the hunt began when Umbridge kicked Dumbledore out of Hogwarts. We know that it takes Dumbledore the better part of a year in HBP to track down the locket Horcrux's original location. Yet in July 1996 (summer between Books 5 and 6), Dumbledore found and destroyed the ring Horcrux. This was not simply good luck—Dumbledore spent his time since leaving Hogwarts in OotP hunting down the ring Horcrux. After all, before Dumbledore leaves we get this little gem: "'Oh no,' said Dumbledore, with a grim smile, 'I am not leaving to go into hiding.'" (OP622) No indeed, Dumbledore is going off to do some Horcrux hunting!

This was the crux of Dumbledore's plan to use the prophecy as a decoy. Dumbledore probably realizes that one of Voldemort's top priorities is killing him. Dumbledore wants to hunt down Horcruxes unmolested (for if Voldemort finds out, that'd defeat the whole purpose). So he had better make extra-sure Voldemort's attention is focused exclusively on something else. The plan works swimmingly—Dumbledore gets several uninterrupted months of Horcrux hunting without anyone being the wiser.

In fact, he was actually planning for something like this. Certainly, he seems prepared when Umbridge discovers the DA and goes on the warpath. Considering how concerned he is about the students of Hogwarts, it seems rather unlike Dumbledore to leave them at Umbridge's mercy just to cover up for Harry and the DA, unless he had something rather important to be doing. And in his little speech to Fudge, Dumbledore indicates that he does have important plans: "I could break out [of Azkaban], of course—but what a waste of time, and frankly, I can think of a whole host of things I would rather be doing." (OP620)

Of course, this is partially Dumbledore being snarky for the heck of it. He has lost all patience with the Ministry, and he no longer politely acquiesces to them the way he did in CoS and PoA. But everything Jo writes is there for a reason, and this statement was her signal that Dumbledore had something important to be doing at the time.

Dumbledore was waiting for an opportunity to be "kicked out" of Hogwarts. He could have stayed if he so wished, but at first opportunity, he invites Fudge and Umbridge to "force" him to go on the run. This makes sense—Dumbledore cannot go Horcrux hunting if it would make Umbridge and Fudge suspicious, but once he saw an opening to leave for a few months, he took it. It just illustrates how crafty Dumbledore is.

And this was the ultimate payoff from the prophecy decoy. Dumbledore has kept Voldemort chasing after the prophecy (with increasing effort) for ten months at this point, from late June 1995 to late April 1996.[39] He was doing research while Voldemort was occupied, and that was very nice, but now he has two months to hunt a Horcrux while Voldemort remains obsessed with the prophecy. All in all, the decoy was a resounding success.

The Occlumency Gamble

Dumbledore may have succeeded in distracting Voldemort with the prophecy for a good long while, but eventually the time ran out because another plan of Dumbledore's had failed: having Harry learn Occlumency. I've said before that Dumbledore likes controlled situations, but in *Order of the Phoenix*, he sends his two most valuable and volatile assets—Harry

---

[39] When the DA was busted, per the *Lexicon*'s calendar.

and Snape—into an emotionally charged situation with more variables than he can hope to control.

Dumbledore genuinely believes that teaching Harry Occlumency himself is the equivalent of hanging a "Welcome Voldemort!" sign in Harry's mind, and Snape is the only other one qualified to teach Harry Occlumency. So Dumbledore does his best to impress upon both parties—as well as upon those adults to whom Harry would listen—the importance of this exercise. But even if by some miracle the personality clash does not completely derail the exercise, there is another danger: Harry breaking into Snape's mind and seeing an awful lot of things he shouldn't.

At this moment in time, thirteen of the twenty memories that will encompass the Prince's Tale are already in Snape's head. While the most revelatory stuff has yet to be said—the fact that Harry's scar is a Horcrux—there is plenty in those first thirteen memories that Dumbledore (let alone Snape) really does not want Harry to see.

It is critical to Snape that Harry not find out about his love for Lily. For one thing, we know that's the reason that Snape's Worst Memory—the one where he calls Lily a Mudblood—is hidden away from Harry. For another, consider the time Harry uses a Shield Charm and ends up seeing Snape's memories:

> Harry's mind was teeming with memories that were not his—a hook-nosed man was shouting at a cowering woman, while a small dark-haired boy cried in a corner.... A greasy-haired teenager sat alone in a dark bedroom, pointing his wand at the ceiling, shooting down flies.... A girl was laughing as a scrawny boy tried to mount a bucking broomstick—
>
> "ENOUGH!" (OP591-592)

THE LIFE AND LIES OF ALBUS DUMBLEDORE 107

One guess as to who that girl laughing was... Lily. Snape lets Harry see his abusive home, but as soon as the scene switches to a memory with Lily, Snape pulls away. He does not want Harry to see the friendship between them. Apart from anything else, Snape knows that Harry is the type to throw Lily's love in his face (Exhibit A: "[My dad] saved your life!" PA285). Snape would never be able to look Harry in the eyes again!

But there's more to it than that: there is one memory Snape has that would scupper all of Dumbledore's plans.

> "The—the prophecy ... the prediction ... Trelawney ..."
>
> "Ah, yes," said Dumbledore. "How much did you relay to Lord Voldemort?"
>
> "Everything—everything I heard!" said Snape. "That is why—it is for that reason—he thinks it means Lily Evans!" (DH677)

The entire point of this Occlumency exercise is to avoid Harry being used to get the prophecy. If he hears Snape and Dumbledore discussing a prophecy about his mother, Harry is not the type to put it out of his mind; he would go tearing away to the Department of Mysteries, straight into the Death Eaters' clutches.

Dumbledore sets up a safety precaution, and loans Snape the Pensieve for the lessons. This is probably not done lightly, given that it contains all of Dumbledore's own memories, but he trusts Snape not to abuse that. Dumbledore needs to protect the knowledge of the prophecy. And to appease Snape, who is doing a task he really does not want to be doing here, Dumbledore ensures he "shall never reveal the best of [Snape]."

(DH679) So Snape ends up with the Pensieve during the Occlumency lessons.

What Dumbledore did not foresee was how the Pensieve actually made it likelier that Harry would see those memories. Snape will take any opportunity to knock Harry down a peg—that's why he makes such a show of removing his memories into the Pensieve every single time. He knew Harry's curiosity would be piqued. This is Snape snidely asserting his dominance over Harry, nonverbally gloating that Snape's memories were safely tucked away whereas all of Harry's were fair game.

Harry is reckless at the best of times. The combination of Voldemort-related mood swings, constant goading from Umbridge, and Snape going through his memories was a cocktail destined to end in disaster. And so it does when Harry takes the opportunity to dive into Snape's forbidden memories.

Snape got lucky that Harry only saw the memory he did. But when Snape finds Harry, he cannot be sure which memories Harry has seen. The one he catches Harry in is squarely in the middle, and if Harry saw the other memories in *The Prince's Tale*, the results would have been catastrophic.

So when Snape blows up at Harry and brings the Occlumency lessons to an inglorious conclusion, it is not just anger we are witnessing.

> It was scary: Snape's lips were shaking, his face was white, his teeth were bared.
>
> "Amusing man, your father, wasn't he?" said Snape, shaking Harry so hard that his glasses slipped down his nose.
>
> "I—didn't—"
>
> Snape threw Harry from him with all his might.

> Harry fell hard onto the dungeon floor.
>
> "You will not tell anybody what you saw!" Snape bellowed.
>
> "No," said Harry, getting to his feet as far from Snape as he could. "No, of course I w—"
>
> "Get out, get out, I don't want to see you in this office ever again!"
>
> And as Harry hurtled toward the door, a jar of dead cockroaches exploded over his head. (OP649-650)

To be sure, Snape is genuinely angry here—Harry just violated his privacy, so Snape bellows and throws dead cockroaches at Harry.[40] But while the text says Snape was "white with rage," his reaction is different from the other times he has a hissy fit (in *Prisoner of Azkaban*, and during "The Flight of the Prince" in HBP). Here he maintains his sarcasm, and at no point is he described as "deranged," "mad," or anything synonymous with that. There's no CapsLock, no italics, only two measly exclamation points! There's more going on in Snape's head at this point than pure fury.

Snape is terrified in this scene, because he realizes how badly he messed up by allowing Harry to get into those memories (and remember, he still doesn't know how much Harry has seen). The physical description of

---

[40] A popular theory online is that this was all an act for Harry's benefit to show him how awful James and Sirius were. (For example, see the chapter discussion for "OP28—Snape's Worst Memory" at the *HP Companion*, https://hp-companion.com/op/op28/) I don't buy this, because Snape must have seven years' worth of memories of being bullied by James and Sirius, so why would he choose the one involving Lily coming to his rescue? Besides, the memory does not cast Snape in a good light either.

Snape at that point—lips shaking, face white—is consistent with fear as well as anger. Snape and Dumbledore had just repaired their relationship less than a year ago, and Snape knows Dumbledore would be livid—he would blame Snape for tempting Harry with those memories. When Snape yells at Harry not to tell anyone about what he saw, it's likely he has Dumbledore in mind, since Snape knows how angry Dumbledore would be after this slipup.

Fortunately for Snape, Dumbledore blames himself (as part of a huge mea culpa at the end of OotP, where Dumbledore shoulders responsibility for almost every bad thing that happened). "I forgot—another old man's mistake—that some wounds run too deep for the healing. I thought Professor Snape could overcome his feelings about your father—I was wrong." (OP833) Dumbledore realizes that the setup of Harry and Snape working together in emotionally fraught conditions, despite any number of precautions, was doomed to fail because of their very natures.

The failure of Dumbledore's gamble on Harry and Snape ends up costing Sirius Black's life, and that has to be awful for Dumbledore. Dumbledore feels guilt acutely, having been consumed by guilt for his sister Ariana's death for a century. Now he can add Sirius's death to his conscience, which is really upsetting for him. However, it's not upsetting enough to stop Dumbledore from going double or nothing on the Harry/Snape gamble.

Repeating Old Plans

There were a lot of balls in the air during *Order of the Phoenix*, so let's recap. The prophecy that everyone spent a year worrying about was essentially of no importance, but only Dumbledore knew this. Dumbledore used the prophecy to send Voldemort on a wild goose chase and used the unwitting Order to keep Voldemort occupied for a year, while Dumbledore started researching and then hunting the Horcruxes. This allowed him a valuable head start on attempting to defeat Voldemort, with no one to bother him.

The evidence indicates that Dumbledore set this plan into motion right away after Voldemort's resurrection, coming up with it on the spot when Harry informed him that Voldemort had returned. Dumbledore spent the night revealing things to Harry about the wands and Crouch Jr. and everything Harry could possibly want to know... except the prophecy. Whatever Dumbledore says to the contrary about not wanting to put Harry through more suffering that night, he certainly didn't seem to shy away from putting Harry through whatever he felt necessary. Dumbledore didn't tell Harry about the prophecy to prevent his secrets from getting leaked—he didn't tell anyone, so as to ensure his decoy worked perfectly. This was the beginning of the Machiavellian Dumbledore we see at work in the last book, and is a harbinger of things to come.

Interestingly, in *Order of the Phoenix*, both Dumbledore and Voldemort revisited their old strategies, and both received an identical result to the last time. In *Sorcerer's Stone*, Dumbledore kept Voldemort occupied by dangling something he wanted in front of him. And just like the *Sorcerer's Stone* served to keep Voldemort busy and mostly harmless for a year, so too did the prophecy. Another commonality: Voldemort failed to acquire both the Stone and the prophecy in the end. This strategy works so well, I bet Dumbledore was half-tempted to give it another go to buy himself another year.

As for Voldemort's strategy, it seems awfully familiar. He exerts a lot of effort to maintain his anonymity from the Ministry. When the Death Eaters are mocking Harry for falling for Voldemort's trap, Harry brings up an excellent point: "Why couldn't

[Voldemort] come and get it himself?" (OP786) And indeed, why not?

Because Voldemort is trying to repeat his plan from the previous year! He uses Harry to achieve an objective, shows off in front of Death Eaters, and maintains anonymity throughout. (This second point probably grew ever more attractive to Voldemort as he spent months doing his own thing with Fudge being none the wiser.) Voldemort wants to display how weak Harry is, that he would fall for a mind trick of Voldemort's. He wants the Death Eaters to bring the prophecy to Voldemort, all while making sure the Ministry is none the wiser. (After all, short of seeing Voldemort in the Ministry, Fudge would keep blaming Dumbledore for everything going wrong.) Just like the previous year, Voldemort takes obstacles out of Harry's path to get him to the goal—I have to believe that the Ministry's security would not allow six teenagers to wander in unmolested in the middle of the night.

This time, however, Voldemort is entirely at fault for the plan going wrong. He completely overestimates his Death Eaters, half of whom are still likely weakened from Azkaban, believing they'll be able to take the prophecy from Harry without incident. To be fair, Voldemort most likely did not expect Harry to show up with six friends in tow (he consistently shows no regard for Harry's friends and allies), and a dozen Death Eaters would have been able to take care of Harry by himself.

It's the same plan as *Goblet of Fire*, and it once again failed because Harry had an ace up his sleeve—Priori Incantatem, love—and Dumbledore was informed immediately. And while the GoF plot at least succeeded in returning Voldemort to his body, Voldemort's OotP plan was an unqualified failure. That's why Voldemort allows his temper to get the better of him when Harry announces the prophecy is smashed, meaning Voldemort will never get to hear its contents. Voldemort really wanted that prophecy, and is so peeved, he throws away his other considerations. He shows up at the Ministry to kill Harry, risking his anonymity, and doesn't even bother waiting for an audience. This time, there are no games or theatrics, he just lets the Killing Curses fly. It's a stark contrast to the Voldemort from Book 4. Yet because Voldemort was so angry as to not listen to Bellatrix hollering about Dumbledore being present, he is surprised by Dumbledore, and utterly defeated—no prophecy, no Death Eaters, and cover blown.

It is after this PR nightmare that Voldemort issues his "I will be the one to kill Harry Potter" decree.[41] We first hear about it from Snape during the "Flight of the Prince": "Have you forgotten our orders? Potter belongs to the Dark Lord—we are to leave him!" (HBP603)

For better or worse, at the end of *Order of the Phoenix*, the schemes of both Dumbledore and Voldemort are over with for that year. Going forward, Dumbledore and Voldemort double down on their respective styles. Voldemort remains a performer throughout the entire series, and his theatricality becomes his predictability (though he learns enough to Avada Kedavra Harry immediately in *Deathly Hallows* and go through the theatrics after the threat has been nullified). Dumbledore, meanwhile, doubles down on his secrets and his manipulation. It's time to reset the chessboard for the final match.

---

[41] This was also probably subtly encouraged by Snape.

Chapter 6:
Albus Dumbledore and the Half-Blood Prince

When we examine Dumbledore's plans for how the war with Voldemort would play out, we can only see the plans he formed in July 1996 onwards. This is because there is a crucial paradigm shift in July 1996: Dumbledore no longer expects to live to see the war effort through. He is blindsided during his hunt for the Ringcrux, when he suddenly gets a blast from the past upon finding it:

> "When I discovered it, after all those years, buried in the abandoned home of the Gaunts—the Hallow I had craved most of all, though in my youth I had wanted it for very different reasons—I lost my head, Harry. I quite forgot that it was now a Horcrux, that the ring was sure to carry a curse. I picked it up, and I put it on, and for a second I imagined that I was about to see Ariana, and my mother, and my father, and to tell them how very, very sorry I was . . ." (DH719-720)

At this point, Dumbledore has not thought about the Hallows in years; certainly not since returning the Cloak to Harry in 1991. But suddenly, the entire chessboard he'd been setting up is upended: he only has a year to live, at most. The odds of the war ending in that year are so long, even Bagman wouldn't bet on it. So Dumbledore has to toss all of his plans out the window, and come up with a whole batch of new plans... and he has the Hallows as a potential confounding variable now.

Until this moment, Dumbledore fully intended to wipe out the Horcruxes single-handedly. After all, who else could do it? Who else has the magical prowess to deal with Voldemort's defenses? Who else has the knowledge of Voldemort's background to figure out what and where the Horcruxes are? And who else has the wherewithal to do it so Voldemort's none the wiser? Ideally, Dumbledore would get rid of all the Horcruxes, deal with the Scarcrux last of all by instructing Harry to sacrifice himself and defeat Voldemort once and for all.

Also until this moment, Dumbledore fully intended to die (much later) as the undefeated master of the Elder Wand. There are conflicting statements in *Deathly Hallows* regarding what Dumbledore intended for the Elder Wand, whether he intended to die undefeated or to pass on mastery of the wand to Snape. Credit here must go to mirrormere's superb editorial, "The Flaw in the Plan,"[42] for untangling the conflicting statements about the Elder Wand. I recommend reading the entire piece, but the gist is that when Harry says the following, they should be read as separate statements instead of interconnected ones.

"Snape never beat Dumbledore! Dumbledore's death was planned between them! Dumbledore

---

[42] http://www.mugglenet.com/2011/01/the-flaw-in-the-plan/ This was the editorial that set me on the path of figuring out Dumbledore's convoluted plans in the last two books. While I disagree with almost all of the conclusions reached, the research is impeccable, and it's exactly the kind of deep dive into the minutiae of Dumbledore's plans that I so enjoy reading.

intended to die undefeated, the wand's last true master! If all had gone as planned, the wand's power would have died with him, because it had never been won from him!" (DH742)

That should be read as:

"Snape never beat Dumbledore! Dumbledore's death was planned between them!" (true)

"Dumbledore intended to die undefeated, the wand's last true master! If all had gone as planned, the wand's power would have died with him, because it had never been won from him!" (true... until Dumbledore realized he would be dying in the middle of the war against Voldemort)

This is Harry getting snappish with Voldemort and not explaining himself properly. Then again, he is not a villain, and therefore not as experienced at monologuing for an audience. What he is attempting to communicate is that Dumbledore originally intended to die undefeated "if all had gone as planned." But when it turned out that Dumbledore would be dying before the war ended, that plan changed.

Choosing a Lieutenant

Anyway, Dumbledore finds out he has a year to live. And this changes everything. Someone else will have to take up the mantle and defeat Voldemort, and Dumbledore will have to split his energies between preparing his replacement and doing all he can now in order to leave less for them to do. So, who should he groom to take over?

Harry seems like the obvious choice in retrospect, but why couldn't someone else have tackled the Horcruxes while Harry concerned himself only with dealing with Voldemort? "McGonagall is a very worthy second in command," Jo once said in an interview.[43] Snape is certainly both capable and cunning, though surely a tad busy playing double duty for two bosses. There's Kingsley, Lupin, Moody, any number of wizards and witches who would take up the mission. As Molly Weasley says, "if Dumbledore needed work doing, he had the whole Order at his command!" (DH88)

In the end, Dumbledore chooses Harry for several reasons, despite his youth and magical inexperience. Harry has experience dealing directly with Voldemort, both from a standpoint of understanding him, and of working through his magical traps. This is, of course, largely by Dumbledore's own design. Recall that in *Sorcerer's Stone*, Dumbledore orchestrated a very elaborate scheme purely to give Harry this valuable experience for the first time. Now, Harry is old hat at fighting Voldemort. When Dumbledore dies, Voldemort is going to have a lot of legroom, and Harry will likely have to be on the run—why not have him doing something useful?

Dumbledore's first order of business is to get to Slughorn, so Slughorn can provide the last crucial piece of information: how many Horcruxes Voldemort has made. And there is no more time to waste, so he deploys Harry, first to get Slughorn to come to Hogwarts, then by setting Harry the task of retrieving the memory. Dumbledore kills two birds with one stone by making Harry get the memory from Slughorn. Not only does it get Dumbledore the memory at long last, it also provides Harry with experience wheedling information about Voldemort from reluctant people.

---

[43] Melissa Anelli and Emerson Spartz, "The Leaky Cauldron and MuggleNet Interview Joanne Rowling," July 16, 2005, http://www.accio-quote.org/articles/2005/0705-tlc_mugglenet-anelli-1.htm.

We see how this comes in handy with the Grey Lady, much later.

A brief aside: Dumbledore finally gives Snape the D.A.D.A. position that Snape has so coveted, for two reasons. First and foremost, Dumbledore is just really desperate to get Slughorn to Hogwarts, so it's necessary to have both Snape and Slughorn teaching. But Dumbledore also knows that if Snape kills him within the year, he won't return to the job afterwards, so he isn't worried about the jinx on the job taking Snape out of the picture prematurely.[44]

Dumbledore knows from Snape that Voldemort "believes the school will soon be in his grasp, yes." (DH682) At this point, Dumbledore had just gotten Hogwarts back from Umbridge's regime, and has seen the damage she wrought: Hagrid attacked and exiled, McGonagall hospitalized, etc. Voldemort would want someone sympathetic running Hogwarts—if one of Voldemort's minions takes over Hogwarts, things would be even worse than they were under Umbridge.

---

[44] Robbie Fischer had an alternate theory for this, pre-DH. In his essay "He Did It All for Harry," http://www.mugglenet.com/2006/01/the-burrow-he-did-it-all-for-harry/, Robbie posits that Dumbledore gave in and assigned Snape the D.A.D.A. position purely to advance Harry's career prospects. Dumbledore knew Harry couldn't become an Auror without taking a Potions N.E.W.T., and Snape wouldn't accept Harry into his N.E.W.T. class. So instead of overriding Snape, Dumbledore shuffled around his entire pedagogical roster to make sure Harry could become an Auror. While I don't buy this theory, I really like it, because it perfectly captures how Dumbledore cares disproportionately for Harry. As Robbie writes, "He left the entire wizarding world more insecure and leaderless than ever, more or less to advance the career prospects of a single, favored student." That statement is right at home in this book.

So Dumbledore creates a contingency plan to protect the students of Hogwarts: have Snape convince Voldemort to appoint him headmaster, so Snape can influence goings-on at Hogwarts. It's not like a lot of his Death Eaters would make particularly good school administrators—Snape seems the obvious choice. Dumbledore asks Snape for "your word that you will do all in your power to protect the students at Hogwarts?" (DH682)

And if Voldemort does not gain control of Hogwarts before the next term starts, it's hard to see Headmistress McGonagall welcoming Snape back to his teaching post after Snape killed Dumbledore. So however it works out, Snape need not worry about getting around the jinx to teach D.A.D.A. a second year.

Dumbledore prepares Harry to be his successor in a number of ways. The most obvious is by giving Harry much of the invaluable knowledge Dumbledore has acquired about Tom Riddle, through the use of the memories in the Pensieve. But also significant is that Dumbledore creates a support network for Harry. He allows Harry to bring Ron and Hermione in on the secrets—a most un-Dumbledore-like move, but a necessary one because Harry will need allies. Dumbledore has been grooming the Trio for this since *Sorcerer's Stone*; in particular, he places a lot of faith in Hermione to be the brains of the operation since she acquitted herself so admirably saving Sirius and Buckbeak in *Prisoner of Azkaban*.

Dumbledore picks up a lesson from Voldemort, Fudge, and Scrimgeour: he invests in making Harry a symbol. He needs to make sure all of his allies will rally to Harry's side when need be. (He also needs a new torch-bearer for the cause, since that was his own role, and who better than the Boy Who Lived and the Chosen One?) We even get a glimpse of how Dumbledore was helping this along—witness this exchange between Kingsley and Lupin: "The last words

Albus Dumbledore spoke to the pair of us!" / "Harry is the best hope we have. Trust him." (DH72)

However, Dumbledore unwittingly handicapped Harry by maintaining his penchant for secrets and lies. It served Dumbledore well in *Order of the Phoenix* to keep everyone in the dark, because Dumbledore is capable of masterminding against Voldemort single-handedly. Harry, on the other hand, could certainly have used the help of powerful adult wizards during his quest. The decision to keep secrets from their followers is something Dumbledore and Voldemort have in common, and Harry follows suit to his detriment.

Dumbledore also keeps up the Horcrux hunt as all this is going on. He knows Voldemort is likely to have made at least one more conventional Horcrux, because there's the perfect candidate: Slytherin's locket. It checks all the boxes—historical Hogwarts artifact, trumpets Voldemort's Slytherin ancestry, is connected to snakes, and is known to have disappeared around Tom Riddle. So Dumbledore begins looking for the next Horcrux,[45] and it takes him all of his last remaining year to find its hiding spot.

But at the end of April, Harry finally has a Felix-Felicis-assisted breakthrough, and gets Dumbledore the memory from Slughorn. Dumbledore finally has the answer to the question that's plagued him for almost two years: Voldemort wanted to make six Horcruxes.

From here on out, it's fairly straightforward for Dumbledore. The diary and ring are gone. Nagini makes three, though she must be the last one destroyed so as not to arouse Voldemort's suspicions. Harry's scar was the unwitting seventh Horcrux, which has a whole separate plan percolating around it. Slytherin's locket and Hufflepuff's cup make five. The

---

[45] Dumbledore admits he doesn't know which specific Horcrux he's hunting (HBP547).

only unknown is the sixth Horcrux, but some psychoanalysis of Voldemort reveals that it's likely a relic of Ravenclaw's.[46] All that's left to do is to hunt down as many of them as possible while still alive, and to show Harry the ropes.

The Last Horcrux Lesson

With so much going on—preparing Harry for the Horcrux hunt, looking for the locket, dealing with new Minister of Magic Rufus Scrimgeour's interference and Slughorn's reticence, and plotting out the rest of the war—Dumbledore makes a mistake, and underestimates a teenage boy to his own peril (sound familiar?). Draco Malfoy is spending the entire year trying to kill Dumbledore and grows increasingly sloppy with his attempts. Dumbledore delegates the Draco problem to Snape and assumes Draco won't actually achieve anything.[47]

Perhaps if Dumbledore had realized the obvious parallels here, he would not have been so blasé about Draco. Consider: a teenage boy is recruited and groomed by the leader of a given side, charged with a suicide mission, the seemingly impossible task of

---

[46] It's rather puzzling why Dumbledore did not get the Grey Lady to spill her secrets the way she did to Harry. Surely he would think it worthwhile talking to her, given that she is Helena Ravenclaw, and is best positioned to know something relevant about her mother's artifacts? We'll have to chalk this one up to being on Dumbledore to-do list for the last month of his life.

[47] There is irony in Draco being assigned to kill Dumbledore as Voldemort's retribution against Lucius. Since Dumbledore orchestrated the entire prophecy decoy that led to the Battle of the Department of Mysteries and Lucius Malfoy's disgrace, Dumbledore is responsible (in a very roundabout way) for Draco being in Voldemort's crosshairs and being charged with killing him.

destroying the opposing side's general.[48] Both teenage boys would receive a crucial bit of assistance from Severus Snape. Yet while Dumbledore had complete faith in Harry succeeding, he did not have as high an opinion of Draco Malfoy.

This results in Dumbledore being extremely cavalier about his ticking clock. He still has not told Harry half of what Harry needs to know about Horcruxes—for example, how to destroy them, which seems a rather crucial point. We can only assume that Dumbledore was planning on showing Harry how to destroy a Horcrux right after they got the locket, preferring to show rather than tell. However, at this point Dumbledore only had a month left to live, which is cutting it rather close.

Dumbledore seemingly staked all his chips on this final Horcrux lesson with Harry, since presumably that's when he would have told Harry about Gryffindor's sword being an ideal tool for destroying Horcruxes. However, since he doesn't get to, it's only sheer dumb luck that saves Dumbledore's plans from going up in flames. Harry gets the sword because Phineas Nigellus overhears where the Trio is camping through his portrait, allowing Snape to go and deliver the sword. It all worked out in the end, but it would have been much more sensible to tell Harry during one of their Horcrux lessons, "By the way, if I should kick

---

[48] Credit here goes to Lady Lupin, who saw this parallel even before *Deathly Hallows* was released. In Spinner's End #10: "The Other Trio: Dark, Darker and Darkest," Lady Lupin wrote the following very prescient passage: "Harry's task is to vanquish Voldemort; Malfoy's task is to kill Dumbledore. Each boy must face the far more experienced leader of the opposing force. In this case, Draco was unable to complete his task, and Snape did it for him. Will Harry complete his task? Will Snape aid Harry in that task?"
http://www.mugglenet.com/2005/12/spinners-end-the-other-trio-dark-darker-and-darkest/

the bucket, grab Gryffindor's sword from my office right away!" I suppose no one's planning is perfect.

Much of the blame for how ill-equipped Harry is to hunt Horcruxes can be put at Draco's feet. Draco managed to get Death Eaters into Hogwarts after all, leading to Dumbledore dying before he'd gotten all his ducks in a row. Of course, Draco interfered in Dumbledore's plans in an even more significant way... stick a pin in that.

We now come to the crux of this entire exercise and must determine what exactly Dumbledore dreamed up during *Half-Blood Prince* to end the war. I must warn you, from this point forth, we shall be leaving the firm foundation of fact and journeying together through the murky marshes of Dumbledore's mind into thickets of wildest guesswork. Figuring out Dumbledore's plans thus far was challenging, because he is brilliant and works off-screen for the most part. But the gist of them can be gleaned with some amount of certainty. Figuring out his ultimate plans for *Deathly Hallows* is a Herculean task that required pages of notes taken from the last three books, the reconciling of myriad contradictions, and the extraction of copious coincidences. From here on in, I may be as woefully wrong as Humphrey Belcher, who believed the time was ripe for a cheese cauldron (HBP197).

Plan A: The Horcruxes

We begin with the most straightforward plans: getting rid of the Horcruxes (including a sacrifice on Harry's part) and defeating Voldemort. Note that these plans are probably all formed during the beginning of *Half-Blood Prince*, as soon as Dumbledore is aware he will not live to see the end of the war play out. After evaluating all of his options, Dumbledore comes up with a plan and a backup plan, both of which rely exclusively on two individuals: Harry and Snape.

THE LIFE AND LIES OF ALBUS DUMBLEDORE

However the end will play out, both plans start with the same few steps.

1. Snape becomes master of the Elder Wand upon killing Dumbledore.
2. Harry destroys all the remaining Horcruxes somehow: the locket, cup, Nagini, and an unknown Horcrux of Ravenclaw's.
3. Harry is alerted to the fact that his scar is a Horcrux.
4. Harry sacrifices himself to destroy the Scarcrux.
5. Harry's willing sacrifice imbues the wizarding world with the same protection that Harry got from Lily's sacrifice, ensuring that Voldemort cannot hurt them anymore.

However, from here events may play out in two different directions. There is one direction that Dumbledore anticipates it going in, and what he hopes for—let's call this Plan A:

6. Because Harry is tethered to life by Voldemort, he should theoretically not die when Voldemort tries to kill him.
7. Harry comes back to life and proceeds to defeat Voldemort.

Dumbledore can be reasonably assured that these first five steps will go according to plan. Let's put the Elder Wand aside for a minute, since that has no bearing on the rest of Plan A. Assuming Harry manages to not get himself killed, he should be able to get rid of the Horcruxes eventually. This destruction of Horcruxes is the top priority, and Dumbledore does not mess with this part of the plan (except for the aforementioned glaring oversight of not getting Gryffindor's sword to Harry in an efficient manner).

Then, once Harry is informed of the Scarcrux, he will doubtless go to sacrifice himself, because that is who Harry is. And the protection spell should work out fine as well.

The complications arise in the last two steps—namely, whether Voldemort tethering Harry to life would be enough to keep Harry actually alive. Recall that Voldemort used Harry's blood to regenerate, and therefore Voldemort's body is helping keep the enchantment of Lily's sacrifice alive. Dumbledore thinks this will keep Harry alive. However, "[Harry] and Lord Voldemort have journeyed together into realms of magic hitherto unknown and untested." (DH710) So Dumbledore cannot be sure whether Harry will live or not.

In fact, Jo stresses that there was no way for Dumbledore to know that Harry would survive being killed by Voldemort. On her old website, she wrote, "It is important to state that I always saw these kinds of magic (the very deepest life and death issues) as essentially un-scientific; in other words, there is no "Elder Wand + Lily's Blood = Assured Survival" formula."[49]

If Harry does survive (the supposed and preferred outcome), he then goes about defeating the newly mortal Voldemort. This would still require prodigious skill, since Lord Voldemort's powers are formidable. But Dumbledore believes it can be done, especially since Harry will have good allies and his trusty phoenix-feather wand with its complex relationship to Voldemort. But defeating Voldemort is of paramount importance, so a contingency plan is needed.

---

[49] https://web.archive.org/web/20110814232616/https://www.jkrowling.com/textonly/en/faq_view.cfm?id=122

It Is Our Choices

Let us revisit Step 5: Harry's *willing* sacrifice imbuing the wizarding world with magical protection from Voldemort. Dumbledore is hoping to invoke the same magic that gave Harry magical protection through Lily's sacrifice, but on a grand scale. The crucial factor for that to work is choice: there must be a choice presented and a choice made for the sacrifice to result in magical protection.

Knowing the power of such magic, Dumbledore has been emphasizing the importance of choices for years. It first comes up in the books' most enduring quote, in *Chamber of Secrets*: "It is our choices, Harry, that show what we truly are, far more than our abilities." (CS333)

Dumbledore revisits the idea in *Goblet of Fire* after Cedric's death: "Remember, if the time should come when you have to make a choice between what is right and what is easy, remember what happened to a boy who was good, and kind, and brave, because he strayed across the path of Lord Voldemort." (GF724)

It's worth noting that every time Dumbledore explicitly brings up the importance of choices, it is always right after he receives a crucial piece of information about Voldemort's Horcruxes. That information serves as a reminder to Dumbledore that he will have to invoke magic based on good choices in order to eliminate the Horcruxes. Or perhaps it's because making Horcruxes is among the worst choices someone can make, and it just brings choices to Dumbledore's mind. Either way, Horcruxes and choices are inextricably linked in the text.

Finishing up the motif, Dumbledore and Harry's final word on choices comes at the end of the final Horcrux lesson, in the chapter titled "Horcruxes," where Dumbledore finally gets the crucial piece of information regarding multiple Horcruxes: that Tom Riddle intended to make seven.

> "It is essential that you understand this!" said Dumbledore, standing up and striding about the room, his glittering robes swooshing in his wake; Harry had never seen him so agitated.
>
> [...]
>
> "In other words, you are free to choose your way, quite free to turn your back on the prophecy! But Voldemort continues to set store by the prophecy. He will continue to hunt you ... which makes it certain, really, that—"
>
> "That one of us is going to end up killing the other," said Harry. "Yes."
>
> But he understood at last what Dumbledore had been trying to tell him. It was, he thought, the difference between being dragged into the arena to face a battle to the death and walking into the arena with your head held high. Some people, perhaps, would say that there was little to choose between the two ways, but Dumbledore knew—and so do I, thought Harry, with a rush of fierce pride, and so did my parents—that there was all the difference in the world. (HBP510-512)

There is not just a moral difference here, there is a magical difference. Intent matters in self-sacrificial magic just as much as it matters in casting Unforgivables: there is powerful magic whose efficacy depends entirely on choice. If Dumbledore intends to utilize this arcane branch of magic, it is imperative that Harry believes he has free will—otherwise, the magic won't work. This is why Dumbledore is so agitated: all his plans rely on Harry's buying in to this concept.

But Dumbledore has done a good job over the years: Harry gets it in the end. As long as Harry is making a conscious choice to "walk into the arena with his head held high," there will be all the magical difference in the world. And that will form the centerpiece of Dumbledore's contingency plan.

Plan B: Snape's Redemption

This plan is concerned with the eventuality of Harry dying by Voldemort's hand. Let us assume the first five steps in Plan A occurred exactly as they would otherwise. Starting after Step 5, this plan diverges from Plan A:

6. Voldemort succeeds in killing Harry.
7. Thanks to the protection from Harry's sacrifice, and the fact that Voldemort's now mortal, another reasonably talented wizard should be able to kill Voldemort.
8. Ideally, Snape uses the Elder Wand to defeat Voldemort, thereby clearing his name.

So let's say Harry does not survive the sacrifice. Upsetting though that would be, Dumbledore has planned for this possibility. If Harry ends up dying, his sacrifice should offer protection for all those on the side of good. Therefore, any of Harry's allies could take up the fight against Voldemort, and since they will be protected from Voldemort's magic, it's reasonable to assume they would be able to defeat Voldemort.

This does not even clash with what the prophecy says—namely, that Harry is the "one with the power to vanquish the Dark Lord." (OP841) In this scenario, Harry was the one with the ability to protect the world from Voldemort, empowering someone else to actually do the vanquishing. And in this case, Harry is the one who dies at the hand of Voldemort, so the prophecy still works out.

Dumbledore must have prepared people for this eventuality, no doubt by telling the most powerful of his allies (like McGonagall and Kingsley) something along the lines of, "Harry will be the one to defeat Voldemort. However, should Harry die, it falls to you to kill Voldemort." At the very least, Dumbledore told Snape this, and he ensured that Snape should be well equipped to kill Voldemort by making Snape the master of the Elder Wand (see Plan A).

If Snape is to be the one to kill Voldemort, he would have had to rely on nothing more than his own prodigious skill. Snape does not have all of the magical protections that Harry has against Voldemort; including a wand imbued with Fawkes's tailfeathers for a core, Harry's enormous courage, and Voldemort's own deadly skill (DH711). So Dumbledore plans to give him the next best thing: the most powerful wand in existence. We've discussed the conflicting language before, but I think it clear that Dumbledore (at some point) intended Snape to have the Elder Wand, so Snape could be the one to defeat Voldemort should Harry fail. This is supported by the following exchange:

> "[Y]ou meant [Snape] to end up with the Elder Wand, didn't you?"
>
> "I admit that was my intention," said Dumbledore (DH721)

This is the first change of plans Dumbledore has regarding the Elder Wand, given that Dumbledore originally meant to die without having the power of the Elder Wand transfer to anyone else. But desperate times call for desperate measures, and Dumbledore not living to see the Voldemort War conclude certainly qualifies. This is the first change of plans, made in the beginning of HBP, but it will not be the last.

The plan for Snape to master the Elder Wand shows just how much faith Dumbledore had in him. He essentially painted a bulls-eye on Snape's back when he conceived of this plan. Dumbledore says he knew Voldemort would go after the Elder Wand (DH721), as soon as he realized that a borrowed wand would not work against Harry's wand. In other words, after the very next time Harry and Voldemort interacted, Voldemort would set out to get the Elder Wand.

Dumbledore knows that Voldemort cannot resist magical MacGuffins when they present themselves (see: Sorcerer's Stone, prophecy). Dumbledore would surely not underestimate Voldemort's intelligence and ability to figure out that Snape was the wand's master.[50] So he put his faith in two things: in keeping Harry away from Voldemort, and in hoping that Snape had enough cunning to keep himself alive once Voldemort does set out on the quest.

As mirrormere astutely pointed out in "The Flaw in the Plan," that first objective could help explain the reasoning behind the wholly idiotic Seven Potters plan—send Voldemort on a wild goose chase after the

---

[50] An internet commenter, CaseyL, offered a different theory: Dumbledore "intended to keep the fact that Snape had killed him secret." (http://disq.us/p/17hr5fd) They claim that Snape would have told Voldemort that Dumbledore died because of his fatal hand injury. It's an interesting theory, supported by Snape telling Narcissa and Bellatrix how Dumbledore "sustained a serious injury." (HBP31) But this seems like too risky a move for Dumbledore—there would almost certainly be Death Eater witnesses to Snape's murder of Dumbledore, and Snape needs to be in Voldemort's good graces, so he has to take credit for the murder.

wrong Harry (gee, sounds familiar) to prevent him finding out that borrowed wands don't work.[51] The second part—believing Snape can stay alive once Voldemort's on the trail—speaks volumes to how highly Dumbledore thinks of Snape's abilities and cunning. But if it were me, I'd forego compliments that come with a death sentence.

This all seems to me the most reckless part of Dumbledore's plan. As previously mentioned, all his plans hinged on keeping two people alive through the war: Harry and Snape. And while he did his utmost to keep Harry alive, he seemingly trusted that Snape would be able to stay alive despite overwhelming odds. This was perhaps his most serious misjudgment, and it was only chance that ended up saving the day at the end.

On the upside, this plan would have offered Snape a chance for redemption should he live long enough to see it through. If Snape defeated Voldemort using the Elder Wand, he would be hailed as a hero by the good side, who would then forgive him for killing Dumbledore. Perhaps this was Dumbledore's small gesture of atonement for the hell he had just sentenced Snape to by requesting Snape kill him—a year of loneliness and exile, devoted to keeping the students as safe as he could with no one but Dumbledore's portrait to talk to.

There is also some beautiful mirroring happening here: if Draco were to fail to kill Dumbledore on Voldemort's orders, Snape would kill Dumbledore for

---

[51] The plan to use Seven Potters seems to me to be some of Jo's weakest writing, because it appears to have arisen out of a desire for drama rather than logic. There are a million easier ways to transport Harry, including even just Polyjuicing Harry into a Weasley and having him anonymously and calmly stroll out of Privet Drive amid a gaggle of redheads.

him (as, indeed, he did.) If Harry were to fail to kill Voldemort on Dumbledore's orders, Snape would kill Voldemort for him. Either way, Snape gets an awful lot of responsibility and risk thrust upon him.

So Dumbledore has his overarching plan ready, and can be reasonably confident in Voldemort's downfall whether Harry lives or not. He prepares Harry to hunt the Horcruxes, and even enlists Ron and Hermione as backups should the unthinkable happen. Thus far, it's all been perfectly logical. Now all he has to do is set the stage for Harry to sacrifice himself. But this is where Dumbledore's emotions got in the way, and he started messing with his plan.

Dumbledore the Machiavellian

Before we continue with Dumbledore's plans, we need to talk about his character. Because all this talk of sacrificing Harry and endangering Snape is a very stark departure from the Dumbledore of the previous books, who was "white as his beard." (DH25) How can this be the same wizard who goes through a lot of hassle to save a condemned hippogriff, who does his best to protect everyone? These are the two Dumbledores I have trouble reconciling.

The death count in the first six books is so comparatively low because Dumbledore works for the good of everyone, rather than for the greater good. . . but in *Deathly Hallows* that's turned on its head. In fact, Jo signals this to us in the first twenty pages of the book, buried in Elphias Doge's sappy obituary: "He died as he lived: working always for the greater good." (DH20) Of course, we as readers interpret this in the benevolent way that Elphias intended, but it foreshadows much of what we come to learn later about Dumbledore.

The deconstruction of the "wise old mentor" archetype in *Deathly Hallows* remains some of Jo's finest work. It's the culmination of a thread running through the latter half of the series: part of growing up is realizing that grown-ups are only human. James Potter and Sirius Black are both knocked off their pedestals. And in the final book, Dumbledore comes crashing down from the biggest pedestal of all.

Dumbledore does not become a villain for a simple reason: given the chance, he will save everyone. That's what reinforces our original impression of Dumbledore in the first six books as one of the ultimate good guys. Dumbledore works tirelessly against Voldemort and to help Harry. The things he does are what's right, no question about it. And that's because he is fortunate enough not to have to make tough choices back then between the greater good and what's good for individuals.

But *Deathly Hallows* presents us with a spectacularly different issue: what happens when there's a very real human cost to the greater good? Voldemort's resurrection is the turning point: with him back in action, it's no longer possible to tie things up in a neat bow for all the good guys. We suddenly realize that Dumbledore is not working to help every single person; rather, he is now sacrificing individuals for the good of all. And this is a much harder pill to swallow.

The first indication we have is Dumbledore's ruthlessness in keeping up the ruse of the prophecy in *Order of the Phoenix*. For those in fandom, that flew under the radar as we busily debated prophecies and Horcruxes and Snape until the last book came out. And talk of Severus Snape... while I hold no great love for him, one paragraph of his dialogue rings unpleasantly true on this topic:

> "You have used me. [...] I have spied for you and lied for you, put myself in mortal danger

> for you. Everything was supposed to be to keep Lily Potter's son safe. Now you tell me you have been raising him like a pig for slaughter—"
> (DH687)

This is it in a nutshell. Dumbledore manipulated Harry only so Harry could (maybe) die when needed; he ruthlessly used Snape's love for Lily to employ Snape as a spy, lying to Snape the entire time about why, and then made Snape a pariah by convincing Snape to kill him. All of this is done elegantly and with impressive ruthlessness, leaving those of us who idolized Dumbledore in quite the moral quandary.

Lorrie Kim makes the point: "Snape had never asked why Dumbledore was protecting Harry." (SNAPE278) In that sense, Snape is suddenly (and bizarrely) the audience surrogate in this scene. Readers, too, never thought to ask why Dumbledore would want to protect Harry—in all the millions of words written analyzing the series before the final book, that question never came up. And that leaves us feeling as betrayed as Severus did at the revelation.

Sure, there is an argument to be made for the necessity of what Dumbledore did, because all of these actions are about bringing Voldemort down. But it's chilling, how much Dumbledore was willing to sacrifice to bring about Voldemort's downfall.

One line Dumbledore says to Harry in *Order of the Phoenix*, when viewed in this light, takes on some sinister layers of meaning: "[Voldemort] hoped, when he possessed you briefly a short while ago, that I would sacrifice you in the hope of killing him." (OP828)

The scary thing is: Voldemort was right. Dumbledore would not have sacrificed Harry in that moment, because he knew it would be ineffective to try killing Voldemort while Horcruxes were out there. But Dumbledore intended to make that move eventually.

For all that Dumbledore makes of Voldemort not understanding love, Voldemort was absolutely correct in his estimation that Dumbledore would sacrifice Harry to kill Voldemort.

Jo sums it up best:

"Although [Dumbledore] seems to be so benign for six books, he's quite a Machiavellian figure, really. He's been pulling a lot of strings. Harry has been his puppet. When Snape says to Dumbledore, 'We've been protecting [Harry] so he could die at the right moment'—I don't think in Book One you would have ever envisioned a moment where your sympathy would be with Snape rather than Dumbledore." [52]

For those unfamiliar with Niccolo Machiavelli's *The Prince*, "Machiavellian" is "the view that politics is amoral and that any means however unscrupulous can justifiably be used."[53] In simpler terms: the ends justify the means—which describes Dumbledore's actions perfectly.

It can be argued that Dumbledore is being utilitarian here, that he is just trying to make things as good as possible for as many people as possible.[54] And for his utilitarian ends, he will sacrifice anything and anyone... including himself. Hardcore fans tend to

---

[52] Shawn Adler, "J.K. Rowling Meets with L.A. Students, Plots Next Move," October 15, 2007, http://www.mtv.com/news/1571977/harry-potter-author-jk-rowling-meets-with-la-students-plots-her-next-move/. Oddly enough, this is the only time Jo has ever mentioned *The Prince*; she has never officially acknowledged it as an influence on HP.
[53] As defined at merriam-webster.com.
[54] For an example of such an argument, read "Dumbledorian Ethics" by Sarah Putnam Park, http://www.the-leaky-cauldron.org/features/essays/issue21/dumbledorianethics/.

bring up the parallel between Dumbledore's death in HBP and the chess match in *Sorcerer's Stone*. Ron, the black knight (Dumbledore), sacrifices himself by allowing the white queen (Snape) to kill him. This leaves the opportunity for Harry to defeat the white king (Voldemort) (SS283).[55]

I think this is a moot point, because Dumbledore does not choose to die when he could have lived. Ever since the Ringcrux's curse affected Dumbledore, he knew he would die within a year. As we've discussed, he nearly runs out the clock on this: the night he actually dies, eleven months are already up, and he is weakened from a nasty potion.[56] Even if by some odd chance he survived the battle against all the Death Eaters, he would still die within a month. So although his death will be for the greater good, he still chooses a death that would be quick and painless for him, and we don't know fully how self-sacrificing he really is.

In fact, here Dumbledore is taking a page right out of *The Prince*: "Those [cruelties] may be called properly used, if of evil it is possible to speak well, that are applied at one blow and are necessary to one's

---

[55] For a much more in-depth analysis of this chess match paralleling the rest of the series, read my essay "The Three-Book-Long Chess Match," http://www.mugglenet.com/2015/01/the-three-book-long-chess-match/. It's part of a series I did about the seven obstacles in *Sorcerer's Stone* serving as an outline for the entire book series.

[56] Talking of the potion in the cave, there is a theory about it buried in LiveJournal by felicitys_mind, which makes a lot of sense. She posits that the potion would make the drinker relive Tom Riddle's torture of Amy Benson and Dennis Bishop, consistent with Voldemort's use of some Horcruxes as a highlight reel of his early triumphs. Harry believes that the potion actually made Dumbledore relive "watching Grindelwald hurting [Aberforth] and Ariana," (DH568) but that is an assumption on Harry's part made without any evidence. https://felicitys-mind.livejournal.com/3530.html

security, and that are not persisted in afterwards." (Chapter VIII)[57] Lorrie Kim, in *SNAPE: A Definitive Reading*, connected this quote and the "cruelties" to Dark magic, and to Dumbledore's request that Snape kill him (SNAPE211).

> "[Severus,] you alone know whether it will harm your soul to help an old man avoid pain and humiliation. [...] I confess I should prefer a quick, painless exit to the protracted and messy affair it will be if, for instance, Greyback is involved. [...] Or dear Bellatrix, who likes to play with her food before she eats it." (DH683)

Kim uses this as evidence that Snape is the titular Prince, since he will be the one using a Killing Curse as necessary. But since the idea is Dumbledore's, since the Killing Curse is necessary to his security, I take it as further evidence that Dumbledore is the Prince.

I don't believe Dumbledore would have sacrificed himself for the cause. Alive, Dumbledore is just about the greatest asset that the side of good has. Therefore, by Machiavellian reasoning, Dumbledore should stay alive at all costs, except perhaps if there's a choice between Harry and Dumbledore. But it never came to that, and Dumbledore sure seems Machiavellian through and through.

In fact, the identity of The Prince of the HP series was one of Jo's cleverest red herrings. When *Half-Blood Prince* was released, the answer seemed obvious: the Half-Blood Prince was the duplicitous Snape, who must have been clearly modeled on Machiavelli's Prince.

---

[57] My reference for *The Prince* is Project Gutenberg, so there are no page numbers, only chapters.
http://www.gutenberg.org/files/1232/1232-h/1232-h.htm

Many an article was written about that; the best to my memory were Andrew Cooper's[58] and B.J. Texan's[59], both titled "Machiavelli's Half-Blood Prince." The theories were very compelling, and "guy out for himself and playing everybody" served as a very appealing third option to "good guy" or "bad guy." But this was an instance of Jo's misdirection at its finest, because how wrong we all were!

In the fandom's defense, part of Snape's character was derived from *The Prince*. The only issue is that Snape was not based on Machiavelli's titular prince but rather on a historical prince who gets a passing mention in Machiavelli's book, Chapter XIX.[60] However, Severus is featured in only three paragraphs of Machiavelli's treatise, so this is not the be-all-end-all answer to relating the two texts. Because going through Machiavelli's instructions, Snape does not

---

[58] http://www.the-leaky-cauldron.org/features/essays/issue9/machiavelli/

[59] http://www.mugglenet.com/2006/04/machiavellis-half-blood-prince/

[60] Long story short, Severus was an emperor in Ancient Rome. Once he became emperor, he was faced with the problem of two rival emperors, Albinus and Niger. Severus played the two against each other. He pretended to ally himself with Albinus to defeat Niger. Once Niger was defeated, Severus accused Albinus of treachery, "sought him out in France, and took from him his government and life." So, a Severus who played two emperors against each other, then betrayed Albinus and killed him... it seemed pretty obvious that this was the inspiration for Snape.
With the hindsight of *Deathly Hallows*, we received yet another compelling clue. Not only did Severus take Albinus's life, but also his government... rather like Snape killing Albus and then becoming Headmaster of Hogwarts. So yes, this was the inspiration for Snape, who was indeed out for himself first and foremost and had no problem playing Albus and Voldemort against each other.

follow them at all, whereas Dumbledore does to a T. Here are some of the more salient examples:

> "Chapter XIX: That One Should Avoid Being Despised or Hated."
>
> Chapter XIX states that "a prince should guard himself as from a rock" against being "mean-spirited"
>
> Chapter XVIII advises, "Therefore it is unnecessary for a prince to have all the good qualities I have enumerated, but it is very necessary to appear to have them. [...] to appear merciful, faithful, humane, religious, upright, and to be so, but with a mind so framed that should you require not to be so, you may be able and know how to change to the opposite."

Dumbledore has a sterling reputation among those who are anti-Voldemort. He is unfailingly considerate and sympathetic. Dumbledore appears to be the great champion of good and to have all these admirable qualities, yet he is willing and able to cast those things aside when necessary.[61]

In his superb essay, Andrew Cooper lays out Machiavelli's advice in layman's terms. He writes,

> [T]he prince's wisdom must allow him to be noble and virtuous so as to be good and respected, but must also know when and how to be shrewd and forceful. [...] The prince must be accountable to no one other than himself, and choose company wisely. He must be unreadable and impenetrable, guarded in advice and true to his word. He must be strong yet cunning, bold yet secretive.

---

[61] Snape, on the other hand, does not seem to take any of Machiavelli's advice to heart: he revels in being mean-spirited, embraces being despised, and never comes across as merciful or humane.

Reading that paragraph, it matches up perfectly with everything we know of Dumbledore. Dumbledore was good and respected, yet he could be shrewd and forceful. Dumbledore is accountable to no one else, as we find out when the Ministry tries to rein him in and Dumbledore responds with cheerful disdain. Dumbledore is unreadable and impenetrable (hence I'm writing this book). Dumbledore is strong, cunning, bold, and (above all) secretive. Check, check, and an emphatic check all around.

In truth, it would appear that the fandom got a bit overeager with connecting *The Prince* to the Half-Blood Prince.[62] *The Prince* was a treatise on how to be an effective leader, which Snape never aspired to be. The key to Snape's character is that he is an agent of leaders, a double agent at that. Over time, "Machiavellian" came to be simplified to reflect anyone who was ruthless and believed the ends justified the means; but it really applies primarily in the context of leadership. So while Snape may be the Half-Blood Prince, inspired by Emperor Severus as described by Machiavelli, Dumbledore is truly Machiavelli's Prince.

What Was He Thinking?

We have now veered from a saintly Dumbledore to a completely ruthless one, but that is not the full story, as we're about to see upon further examination of Dumbledore's master plans. We have already nitpicked at a few of Dumbledore's more questionable decisions preparing Harry and Snape for their final moves in the war. But as anyone who has devoted hours to discussing *Deathly Hallows* knows, that is just the tip of the iceberg. Unlike the other books, where things happen for a reason by and large, *Deathly*

---

[62] I absolve myself of any blame here; I was fourteen when Andrew Cooper's essay was published!

Hallows seems to be teeming with coincidences that ricochet off each other, with things then working out through sheer dumb luck. It's certainly made my job here much harder than it was for previous books.

One thing in particular does not seem to add up. Considering how desperate Dumbledore was to see Voldemort defeated, considering the prices he was willing to pay to see it done, it just seems like he should have been much more thorough about it. At first glance, he seemed to leave an awful lot to chance... and that's not the Dumbledore we know.

Dumbledore's plan reaches its climax when Nagini is the last remaining Horcrux, which Snape will realize "when Lord Voldemort stops sending that snake forth to do his bidding, but keeps it safe beside him under magical protection." (DH686) At this point, Snape has to find Harry and show him the memories that will inform Harry that he needs to die. There are so many potential disasters in this plan, it's ludicrous.

What if Nagini is not the last remaining Horcrux? What if Harry somehow manages to kill her before finding Ravenclaw's relic? Voldemort won't be as worried for Nagini, given his other Horcruxes, and Snape won't know to do anything.

If Snape is needed at Hogwarts, and Voldemort is to be kept away from Hogwarts, how will Snape even know what's going on with Nagini?

What if Snape doesn't find Harry? Surely the two won't be hanging out on a regular basis.

Why would Harry listen to Snape or look through his memories? If Snape were alive, I'm fairly certain Harry would not have taken Snape's memories... not without a lot of convincing.

What if Harry doesn't have a Pensieve ready when he does get the memories? There's a lot of emphasis on how rare they are. So is he meant to just take Snape at his word, then?

What if Snape dies?!? There is no contingency plan that we know of. No one else knows Harry needs to die. The entire thing goes to hell.[63]

All things considered, about a dozen fortuitous coincidences have to occur for Dumbledore's plan to actually work. This haphazard manner is such a departure from the Dumbledore of previous books that I didn't know what to make of it at first. If Dumbledore is willing to sacrifice so much to defeat Voldemort, he should be absolutely certain of his plan working. Instead, Dumbledore seems to be treating the entire war as a rather amusing game. It doesn't gel with everything we know about Dumbledore. Whether he is benign or cold and calculating, Dumbledore has never before left things up to chance. Why does he not appear to have his bases covered?

The Flaw in the Plan

Dumbledore bares his soul to Harry the most in the climax of *Order of the Phoenix*, when he is talking

---

[63] Admittedly, there could have been yet another contingency plan in place should Snape die, and we just received no indication of it. However, one wonders who would be the backup to Snape's role? It's not in McGonagall's character to deal with murky moral decisions like this; Remus and the Weasleys would lose their minds if told to sacrifice Harry; Aberforth is having none of it; and this isn't the sort of assignment one wants to give a random Order member.
My best guess is that the final contingency plan was Mad-Eye Moody. He seems to be as close to a friend and peer as Dumbledore has. Moody is one of the few people on the Order's side who would have the stomach to make Harry sacrifice himself. Perhaps Dumbledore confided some key knowledge in Moody as a failsafe for Snape. Either way, it's a moot point because Moody is killed at the beginning of *Deathly Hallows*, eliminating the possible contingency plan.

about the prophecy and his plan to take care of Harry. This very illuminating quote emerges from that conversation:

> "Do you see, Harry? Do you see the flaw in my brilliant plan now? I had fallen into the trap I had foreseen, that I had told myself I could avoid, that I must avoid. [...] I cared about you too much," said Dumbledore simply. "I cared more for your happiness than your knowing the truth, more for your peace of mind than my plan, more for your life than the lives that might be lost if the plan failed." (OP838)

It seems to me as if this entire quote can be applied to two plans. The first—the one Dumbledore speaks of in context—is to tell Harry about the prophecy and about his destiny to defeat Voldemort. However, taken out of context this quote can apply almost exactly to Dumbledore's other grand plan: that of Harry sacrificing himself so the Scarcrux is destroyed.

Once Dumbledore began suspecting that Harry has a bit of Voldemort's soul in him (at the end of *Goblet of Fire*), Dumbledore must have realized that Harry would have to die in order for Voldemort to be killed. When Harry relates how Voldemort used his blood to regenerate, Dumbledore has an infamous "gleam of triumph" in his eyes (GF696). This meant that Voldemort had tethered Harry's life to his own. By using Harry's blood to regenerate, which included Lily's protective charm, he ensured that Harry would not be killed by Voldemort should it come to that. In other words, Dumbledore now had hope that Harry might survive the destruction of the Scarcrux.

However, there was no guarantee. All of this magic was completely unprecedented, and Dumbledore confesses that he only "guessed" at all of this (DH710). So Dumbledore still believed that, when the time came, there was a very real possibility that Harry would die.

But when the time came for Dumbledore's scheming and plotting, when he set up a course for Harry to follow after learning that he (Dumbledore) only had a year to live, he fell into the exact same trap. He cared too much about Harry and wanted to delay the moment when Harry might have to die.

This quote also gives the reason why he did not tell Harry of his upcoming sacrifice. Surely by the end of HBP, Harry had proven himself to be exceptionally selfless, and he would have embraced his mortality. Dumbledore argues that "Harry must not know, not until the last moment, not until it is necessary, otherwise how could he have the strength to do what must be done?" (DH685) This is very feeble reasoning indeed, coming from someone who has watched Harry as closely as Dumbledore did. His high opinion of Harry must have made it clear that Harry would, in fact, do what was needed. Dumbledore was nearly thwarted once before by underestimating Harry way back in *Sorcerer's Stone*, when Harry managed to get the Stone out of the Mirror. It's unlikely he'd repeat that mistake.

But Dumbledore "cared more for [his] happiness than [his] knowing the truth, more for [his] peace of mind than [the] plan." Otherwise, Dumbledore would have informed Harry of the sacrifice that was needed, and Harry would have proceeded as necessary.

Dumbledore cared "more for [Harry's] life than the lives that might be lost if the plan failed." This statement is touching in the context of *Order of the Phoenix*, because the only life that has been lost thus far is Sirius's—which is tragic in its own right but is only one person. But when that statement is applied to the grander plan, it takes on a quite sinister tone. Dumbledore was gambling hundreds of lives, he was gambling the entire future of the wizarding world, in order to keep Harry alive and happy a little longer.

And it really was an "all in" gamble, because Dumbledore was gambling both Plan A and Plan B. Plan A (Harry's self-sacrifice doesn't actually kill him, allowing him to beat Voldemort) is defunct if Harry tries to kill Voldemort while the Scarcrux still tethers Voldemort to life. Plan B (Harry's self-sacrifice imbues everyone with magical protection, so someone else beats Voldemort) is defunct if Harry never intends to sacrifice himself, because then no one will have the magical protection against Voldemort. Voldemort's would-be vanquisher would be up against all of his formidable skill with no extraordinary protection as a defense. Dumbledore risked this all on a dangerous gamble for Harry's sake.

Perhaps Dumbledore was Machiavellian, but when it came to Harry, he was very reluctantly so. Or to put it another way, Harry's happiness was an end for Dumbledore that justified almost any means... superseded only by the need to defeat Voldemort once and for all.

So Dumbledore's emotions got in the way. In late February, he has a heated exchange with Snape and tells Snape to come to his office. By this point, Dumbledore has had three private lessons with Harry, and has grown ever fonder of the boy. During that third lesson, Harry relates without a trace of irony how he told the Minister of Magic he was "Dumbledore's man through and through"—a statement that nearly reduced Dumbledore to tears (HBP357). So it is with an exceedingly heavy heart that Dumbledore amends his plans one final time and comes up with two new plans to supplement Plan A and Plan B.

Plan C: Procrastinating Harry's Pain

If you'll recall Plan A, it seems to be well thought out and sensible in its execution, with the glaring exception of Step 3: alerting Harry to the need for his death. As we've discussed, the only reason for Dumbledore not telling Harry this in *Half-Blood Prince* was to keep Harry happy. However, the way in which Harry is finally told is so convoluted that I can only assume it was designed to be intentionally so. Anything else is an insult to Dumbledore's intelligence, because there are a million ways in which he could have told Harry. But this is what Dumbledore chooses to do instead, as dictated to Snape:

> "Harry must not know, not until the last moment, not until it is necessary, otherwise how could he have the strength to do what must be done? [. . .] There will come a time when Lord Voldemort will seem to fear for the life of his snake. [. . .] If there comes a time when Lord Voldemort stops sending that snake forth to do his bidding, but keeps it safe beside him under magical protection, then, I think, it will be safe to tell Harry." (DH685-686)

The step of telling Harry about the Scarcrux should have been wholly independent of whatever else was going on. Instead, Dumbledore slows it down by falsely necessitating three things, in a separate Plan C:

1. Voldemort has to find out that Harry is hunting Horcruxes. Otherwise, he will not fear for Nagini and keep her close, so Snape will not know to alert Harry.

2. After Voldemort is worried for Nagini, Snape has to become aware of this.
3. Snape then has to find a way of getting to Harry and letting him know about the sacrifice.

Ignoring the problem of how Snape will get Harry to listen to him, these three points are a dangerous gamble, but not an absurd one... upon making several assumptions.

i. Voldemort will only find out about Harry's Horcrux hunt after Harry has destroyed all the Horcruxes but Nagini. Otherwise, Harry is royally screwed. But since the whole plan goes to pieces if Voldemort finds out about the Horcrux hunt, and it's extremely unlikely Harry will be able to kill Nagini without alerting Voldemort, this seems like a fair assumption to make.

ii. After learning of the Horcrux hunt, Voldemort will have an opportunity to chat with Snape. Also reasonable, since Voldemort will likely start marshalling all his Death Eaters in his paranoia about Harry hunting Horcruxes.

iii. After learning of the Horcrux hunt, Voldemort will not have the opportunity to make additional Horcruxes. This is the biggest logical flaw in all of this, since it seems like Voldemort would immediately start making more Horcruxes upon finding that the existing ones have been destroyed. It appears that here, Dumbledore was counting on Voldemort's vanity and weakness for drama to save the day... he counted on Voldemort wanting to make grand and powerful objects into Horcruxes, using significant deaths, and this would have slowed Voldemort down considerably. Still, it seems like a risky assumption.⁶⁴

iv. After Snape has seen Nagini's new protected status, he will have the opportunity to talk to Harry before things come to a head. Tricky, since Snape and Harry won't be spending lots of quality time together, but feasible considering Snape's resourcefulness.

In other words, Dumbledore is relying on a very precise sequence of events occurring within a fairly narrow timeline for all of this to work. But evidently, Dumbledore was willing to deal with the risk if it meant prolonging Harry's happy obliviousness. Dumbledore is risking everything just to buy Harry that peace of mind while he's hunting Horcruxes, orchestrating it so he does not find out about the Scarcrux until the very last possible moment.

However, this plan nearly falls apart because the first assumption is false. You know what they say about assuming... safe to say, this is as good a cautionary tale as any. Assumption (i) was that Voldemort would find out about Horcruxes after only Nagini was left... however, he finds out when the Diademcrux is still in play. In other words, the timeline narrows exponentially because Harry now must locate and destroy the Diademcrux before Voldemort has the chance to make new ones, amidst everything else going on.

As if that isn't bad enough, something completely unforeseen happens: the final Horcrux ends up

---

⁶⁴ It's unclear whether there's a limit on splitting one's soul, so it's possible Dumbledore relied on that. When Ron ventures the possibility of Voldemort creating more Horcruxes, Harry says, "Didn't Hermione say he had pushed his soul to the limit already?" However, Ron has a very valid rebuttal: "Yeah, but maybe he doesn't know that." (DH282)

residing at Hogwarts... where Snape is! Thus, the timeline of Dumbledore's carefully crafted plan narrows to mere hours. I'm sure Dumbledore never, in his wildest dreams, thought that Harry would be destroying the last Horcrux and Nagini and sacrificing himself the very same night.

From here on out it's just incredible luck that things work out so Snape ends up delivering the information to Harry, albeit via Pensieve, which I don't think Dumbledore intended (and it was certainly very silly if he did). This plan of Dumbledore's to stall until the moment Harry had to find out about the Scarcrux very nearly sent all of his plans up in flames... But that wasn't the only questionable plot brewing in Dumbledore's brilliant mind.

Enter the Hallows

There is a curiosity about *Deathly Hallows*—namely, why bother with the titular Hallows at all? After all, the Hallows don't have much bearing on the battle between Voldemort and Harry, with the exception of the Elder Wand. Harry unites them and becomes master of Death, but that does not turn out to mean much. As Dumbledore explains, "the true master does not seek to run away from Death. He accepts that he must die, and understands that there are far, far worse things in the living world than dying." (DH721)

So finding the Hallows turned out to be about Harry accepting he must die? Sorry, this reader doesn't buy it. If we know anything about Harry, it's that he would be willing to die with or without Hallows. It seems like there isn't that much special about being master of Death—after all, Lily and James both accepted they must die, and so did Dumbledore, and so did many other people... are they all masters of Death? And if so, then the Hallows are indeed superfluous.

I've yet to find any other theories on why the Hallows are even there, except a few cynical fans who ascribe their presence to Jo's desire for an eleventh-hour MacGuffin. We have dived too far down the rabbit hole to doubt her now, so there is indeed a reason for their inclusion.

Most of what Dumbledore says in his final conversation with Harry can be taken at face value. But there is one statement that stands out as his usual enigmatic half-truth: "I too sought a way to conquer death." (DH713) Dumbledore is not only referring to himself in his youth. I think Dumbledore intended to use the Hallows to make Harry the master of Death in the traditional way—making Harry unable to die.

Did Dumbledore really believe that to be master of Death meant to be a "Master. Conqueror. Vanquisher." as Xenophilius Lovegood says? (DH410) He probably did not believe that it was certain, or even likely, to do so. But what if, on the odd chance, the Hallows did make Harry master of Death in the immortal sense? Dumbledore is so determined to keep Harry alive if at all possible, he is clutching at straws, so he would gamble on odds as long as these.

This is a classic Dumbledore plot, killing two birds with one stone. Not only would he be giving Harry a better chance of survival, but he would also prolong Harry's life quite a bit by sending him hunting for the Hallows instead of the Horcruxes. He could have told Harry about the Hallows, instead of dropping the symbol in *The Tales of Beedle the Bard* and hoping the Trio figured it out. But Dumbledore is a big believer in sending people chasing after things in order to stall them, as we see with Voldemort. He did a similar thing with Harry and the Hallows.

This seems uncharacteristically reckless of Dumbledore, but he essentially confesses as much, when he tells Harry he "counted on Miss Granger to slow [Harry] up." (DH720) So Dumbledore intentionally sent Harry on a time-consuming quest for the Hallows, because it would prolong Harry's life, and it might give him a better chance at survival. This almost seems like the childish procrastination of a student, but it makes sense.

So it turns out that what Harry (and many readers) took as evidence that Dumbledore didn't care—that he sent Harry on a quest with barely any of the needed information—was actually the strongest expression of Dumbledore's love. Harry laments, "I don't know who he loved, Hermione, but it was never me. This isn't love, the mess he's left me in." (DH362) As usual, Hermione is right and Harry's wrong, and Hermione says, "He loved you. I know he loved you."

Dwelling on Dreams

What's interesting is that though Dumbledore intended Harry to master the Hallows, he did not allow Harry to access the Resurrection Stone during his quest. The Stone remained hidden inside Harry's first Snitch, until Harry informed the Snitch that he was about to die. Dumbledore gives us some insight on why he barred access to the Stone:

> "Harry, I only feared that you would fail as I had failed. I only dreaded that you would make my mistakes. I crave your pardon, Harry. I have known, for some time now, that you are the better man." (DH713)

and

> "I was afraid that your hot head might dominate your good heart. I was scared that, if

THE LIFE AND LIES OF ALBUS DUMBLEDORE 153

> presented outright with the facts about those tempting objects, you might seize the Hallows as I did, at the wrong time, for the wrong reasons. If you laid hands on them, I wanted you to possess them safely." (DH720)

This shows that Dumbledore did still have the big picture in mind, despite how derailed his plans were by this point. He wanted to delay Harry and arm him, but he was not willing to risk Harry just getting caught up with the dead and ignoring his Horcrux-hunting duties forever. To be fair to Dumbledore, this is a reasonable concern, because Harry has shown a fascination with death, and upon Dumbledore's untimely end, the temptation may have overpowered Harry. We see how quickly Harry decides that the Stone is the Hallow he'd most like to have (DH414). Only once Harry had fulfilled his mission and was facing his death would Dumbledore allow him to indulge and seek comfort from the deceased.

This comes back to the point I made earlier: for Dumbledore, Harry's happiness and survival is a primary goal, superseded only by the need to defeat Voldemort. Dumbledore does an awful lot for Harry's sake, as I've been expounding. However, he will not give Harry the Resurrection Stone until the last possible moment, because he believes Harry's fascination with death would be the undoing of all his plans if indulged.

In fact, Dumbledore is so confident in the possibility that Harry would be unable to proceed if given the Stone, Dumbledore removes his own ability to help from beyond the grave. Harry says right away that he wants the Stone to "bring people back, [...] Sirius... Mad-Eye... Dumbledore... my parents...." (DH416) Imagine how much easier *Deathly Hallows* would have been if Harry could have brought

Dumbledore back for a chat. But Harry might completely lose himself in his desire to be with the dead, as the second brother in Beedle's tale did, and as Harry nearly does at Godric's Hollow (DH329). Even Dumbledore, who took many risks, will not take this risk: that Harry will dwell on dreams and forget to live.

Plan D: Mastering the Hallows

We know Dumbledore planned for Harry to master the Hallows, because otherwise there's no reason to leave Hermione *The Tales of Beedle the Bard* and little reason to leave Harry the Resurrection Stone. Of course, there seems to be an error here: how could Dumbledore have planned for Harry to master the Hallows when he only mastered the third one by defeating Draco, which wasn't part of the plan at all? Because while the end result was the one intended, everything else in this plan went spectacularly wrong. But before we analyze what went wrong, let's outline Dumbledore's final plan.

1. Leave Hermione *The Tales of Beedle the Bard*, sending the Trio on the hunt for the Hallows rather than the Horcruxes.
2. Leave the Elder Wand in Dumbledore's tomb. Hope that Voldemort won't seek it out for a while, and that it will take Voldemort considerable time to trace the Elder Wand back to Dumbledore.
3. Bequeath the Resurrection Stone to Harry, but encased within the Snitch, ensuring he cannot get to it until the time is right.
4. During their heart-to-heart about Harry having to die, Snape also allows Harry to Disarm him, thereby making Harry the master of the Elder Wand. While the wand itself is still hopefully safe

in Dumbledore's tomb, Harry will open the Snitch, and therefore be master of all three Hallows.

These are the four steps Dumbledore had in mind to make Harry Master of Death before he is about to die. I will admit the last one is pure conjecture, but it makes sense when put along with everything else. After all, how else was Harry supposed to master the wand, if the working theory was that Snape would be its master upon killing Dumbledore?[65]

Note that Dumbledore did not plan for Harry to actually use the Resurrection Stone, or the Elder Wand, only to own them. In this new plan, the wand is better off in Dumbledore's tomb, where it will hopefully stay forevermore and cease causing havoc.

HufflepuffSam wrote otherwise in their essay "The Master of Death,"[66] that to be Master of Death one had to possess all the Hallows, not just be their rightful owner. They claim that for all we know, being Master of Death would render one immortal just as Xenophilius says—but since no one actually possesses all three Hallows at any point, no one ended up being Master of Death.

The only issue with this theory is the question of why the Elder Wand ended up in Dumbledore's tomb. If the plan was for Harry to be given it by Snape, why wouldn't Snape remove it from the tomb? Since there seem to have been no plans in place for Harry to actually have the wand, it appears that Dumbledore thought being the wand's master would suffice.

---

[65] We are still a touch murky on the laws of wand allegiance, so it's possible that a wand would recognize an intentional transfer, like Snape merely giving the wand to Harry. But given the Elder Wand's violent tendencies, that seems implausible at least in this case.

[66] http://www.mugglenet.com/2012/03/the-master-of-death/

Step 4—making Harry the Master of Death—may be the least provable part of this section, but it seems to me to be the only thing that makes sense. Dumbledore talks in the "King's Cross" chapter as if his plan all along has been for Harry to be Master of Death, but he certainly did not plan for Draco to ever be the master of the Elder Wand, and he definitely didn't count on Harry wrestling Draco for wands. Also, considering all the trouble Dumbledore went to in order to have the Trio pursue the Hallows, it seems a waste if Harry wasn't meant to master the wand in the end—then the only added benefit would be Harry's moment of comfort on the way to death. While I think Dumbledore intentionally delayed the Trio to put off the moment Harry has to sacrifice himself, he would not send them on a wild goose chase at so pivotal a time.

Of course, the implications of Step 4 are enormous. The biggest one is that Dumbledore essentially scrapped the last part of Plan B—where Snape is exonerated by defeating Voldemort with the Elder Wand. The rest of Plan B was still in place—where Snape hopefully defeats Voldemort, or at any rate someone does. But Dumbledore took away Snape's most important tool for the job so Harry would stand a slightly better chance of surviving.

The Tragedy of Snape

The timing of when Plan D was formed is a touch unclear. We know Plans A and B (defeating Voldemort) were formed pretty much immediately after Dumbledore got the Ringcrux; we know that Plan C (procrastinating the Scarcrux) was formed in early 1997 because Dumbledore probably gave Snape his instructions soon after he thought of them. Plan D—mastering the Hallows—could have been formed at any point between the two.

We know it was some time after Plan B was formed, because Dumbledore definitely intended Snape to end up with the Elder Wand at some point as we've discussed, and now no longer did. The wand would only be useful to Snape if he was still its master when the dust settled. Since he was no longer intended to be, there was no reason for him to keep custody of it, since then Voldemort might find it more easily. Thus, the wand was to stay in Dumbledore's tomb.

This means Snape has the worst of both worlds. By killing Dumbledore and mastering the wand, the bulls-eye is still on Snape's back. However, he now no longer even gets the benefit that accompanies mastering the wand, since he is to relinquish that to Harry. Dumbledore is once again displaying the enormous faith he has in Snape, since my guess is that Snape is still meant to defeat Voldemort should Harry die, but he is now expected to do so armed with an ordinary wand.

Let's assume that Dumbledore had come up with this by February and informed Snape about allowing Harry to Disarm him along with his other instructions to tell Harry about the Scarcrux—we have no guarantee of this, but it makes things more poetic. Because if one keeps all of this baggage in mind, the scene becomes even more heart-breaking than it already is:

> Dumbledore took a deep breath and closed his eyes.
>
> "Tell him that [. . .] while that fragment of soul, unmissed by Voldemort, remains attached to and protected by Harry, Lord Voldemort cannot die."
>
> [. . .]

> "So the boy . . . the boy must die?" asked Snape quite calmly. [. . .] "I thought . . . all those years . . . that we were protecting him for her. For Lily."
>
> "We have protected him because it has been essential to teach him, to raise him, to let him try his strength," said Dumbledore, his eyes still tight shut. "[. . .] If I know him, he will have arranged matters so that when he does set out to meet his death, it will truly mean the end of Voldemort."
>
> Dumbledore opened his eyes. Snape looked horrified.
>
> "You have kept him alive so that he can die at the right moment? [. . .] You have used me. [. . .] I have spied for you and lied for you, put myself in mortal danger for you. Everything was supposed to be to keep Lily Potter's son safe. Now you tell me you have been raising him like a pig for slaughter—"
>
> [. . .]
>
> Dumbledore watched [the doe] fly away, and as her silvery glow faded he turned back to Snape, and his eyes were full of tears.
>
> "After all this time?"
>
> "Always," said Snape. (DH686-687)

Note Dumbledore's mannerisms: he can barely look Snape in the eye as he says all this. At this point, Dumbledore is speaking of Harry's sacrifice—a supremely painful topic for both parties. But he also knows that he is condemning the man in front of him— the man whom he has worked alongside for sixteen years, who has just displayed the best part of himself—to a wretched existence and to being a target for Lord Voldemort... all while invalidating Snape's motivation for half of his life. As ruthless as Dumbledore is, one has to imagine he feels some guilt here.[67]

In fact, there is a sinister symmetry to Dumbledore's actions here. Twenty years prior, he placed a lower value on Snape's life than on Sirius Black's. Now, even after all that has passed between the two men, Snape's life is still worth less than a promising Gryffindor's—Harry's.

It's even more tragic from the perspective of Snape, both for Dumbledore's betrayal and the fact that all his work in protecting Harry was for naught. This seems incredibly cruel of Dumbledore with regard to Snape, but it is not out of character. The only person Dumbledore truly cares about is Harry. Snape is a useful tool and a valued ally, but no more. We have seen Dumbledore choose Harry over Snape before, in *Prisoner of Azkaban*. Now he does so again, when the stakes are so much higher. Dumbledore pours all of his resources into helping Harry. Meanwhile, he makes Snape an outcast by having Snape kill him, puts Snape into deadly situations on a regular basis, mercilessly

---

[67] Dumbledore's guilt here may explain why he seemed momentarily tempted, several months later, to reveal the truth about Snape to Harry. When Harry is raging about Snape selling out his parents to Voldemort, "Dumbledore did not speak for a moment; he looked as though he was trying to make up his mind about something." (HBP549) After the emotionally charged year Dumbledore has had, he is momentarily tempted to reveal Snape's true colors to Harry, perhaps to alleviate the loneliness and judgment to which he is sentencing Snape. But in the end, Dumbledore chooses to respect Snape's wishes and keep his secret.
On an unrelated note, the fact that the setting sun cast a "bloody tinge" on Dumbledore's face in this scene is an awesome bit of foreshadowing (HBP548).

exploits Snape's love for Lily in order to help Harry, and makes Snape Voldemort's eventual #1 target by making him the master of the Elder Wand. While I hold very little love for Snape, even I pity him for this.

This sheds new light on the scene where he kills Dumbledore. Bellatrix told Harry, "You need to mean [the Unforgivables]!" (OP810) When Snape kills Dumbledore, "there was revulsion and hatred etched in the harsh lines of his face." (HBP595) Snape has every reason to hate Dumbledore. Dumbledore made Snape a pariah among wizards and a target for Voldemort in one fell swoop. Dumbledore intended for Lily's son to die, making a mockery of the last fifteen years of Snape's life. For good measure, Snape probably called forward all the lingering feelings of resentment after the Sirius-and-Moody debacle three years ago. Snape was more than capable of mustering up enough anger to kill Dumbledore, after all that their relationship had gone through over the years.

Having a Choice

A key factor in all of Dumbledore's plans is that everyone—but specifically Harry and Snape—act of their own free will. The things he asks of them are not things that can be forced; Dumbledore has no use for things like Unbreakable Vows. Rather, Dumbledore makes sure that there is a clear right choice to make, and relies on Harry and Snape to make said right choice.

We first see Dumbledore's framing in his second lesson with Harry about Tom Riddle's past. Dumbledore delineates the importance of choice in creating the dichotomy between Harry and Voldemort: they are foils not through only their own choices, but through the opposite choices their mothers made.

> "[Merope] wouldn't even stay alive for her son?"
>
> Dumbledore raised his eyebrows. "Could you possibly be feeling sorry for Lord Voldemort?"
>
> "No," said Harry quickly, "but she had a choice, didn't she, not like my mother—"
>
> "Your mother had a choice too," said Dumbledore gently. "Yes, Merope Riddle chose death in spite of a son who needed her, but do not judge her too harshly, Harry. She was greatly weakened by long suffering and she never had your mother's courage." (HBP262)

This is the template for how Dumbledore presents choices to Harry and Snape. It is genuinely a choice, and is not made by fear of Dumbledore's judgment: he will not be harsh either way, for he understands the chooser's limitations. However, there is a right choice, and the consequences of making the wrong choice are dire: in this example, the existence of Voldemort and all the damage he has wrought.

We see the fruit of Dumbledore's conditioning in the end of *Deathly Hallows*, in events split by two years but only two chapters. But Harry and Snape make the right choice, and in both instances Dumbledore stresses that they do have a choice.

First up is Snape, who is not impressed with the idea of killing Dumbledore, particularly when reminded that killing tears the soul apart.

> "And my soul, Dumbledore? Mine?"
>
> "You alone know whether it will harm your soul to help an old man avoid pain and

> humiliation," said Dumbledore. "I ask this one great favor of you, Severus, because death is coming for me [. . .] I confess I should prefer a quick, painless exit to the protracted and messy affair it will be if, for instance, Greyback is involved [. . .] Or dear Bellatrix, who likes to play with her food before she eats it." (DH683)

Dumbledore lays out compelling evidence in favor of the right answer. But this is all about Snape's views. Only if Snape believes he is performing an act of mercy will his soul be unharmed by the act, and no amount of absolution from Dumbledore can compensate for that.

And when Dumbledore goes through the same exercise with Harry, that one is for all the marbles.

> "I've got to go back, haven't I?"
>
> "That is up to you."
>
> "I've got a choice?"
>
> "Oh yes." Dumbledore smiled at him. "We are in King's Cross, you say? I think that if you decided not to go back, you would be able to . . . let's say . . . board a train."
>
> "And where would it take me?"
>
> "On," said Dumbledore simply.
>
> Silence again.
>
> "Voldemort's got the Elder Wand."
>
> "True. Voldemort has the Elder Wand."
>
> "But you want me to go back?"
>
> "I think," said Dumbledore, "that if you choose to return, there is a chance that he may be

THE LIFE AND LIES OF ALBUS DUMBLEDORE

> finished for good. I cannot promise it. But I know this, Harry, that you have less to fear from returning here than he does."
>
> Harry glanced again at the raw-looking thing that trembled and choked in the shadow beneath the distant chair.
>
> "Do not pity the dead, Harry. Pity the living, and above all, those who live without love. By returning, you may ensure that fewer souls are maimed, fewer families are torn apart. If that seems to you a worthy goal, then we say good-bye for the present." (DH722)

Dumbledore is leading the witness here, but he keeps stressing that it is Harry's choice. Dumbledore presents Harry with objective facts that present a very compelling case for Harry to go back. He talks of "fewer souls maimed" and "fewer families torn apart"—in different words, he is saying exactly what he said three years earlier: "When you have to make a choice between what is right and what is easy, remember what happened to a boy who was good, and kind, and brave, because he strayed across the path of Lord Voldemort." (GF724)

Just as Dumbledore refused to actually tell Snape that it would not tear his soul to perform a mercy killing, he refuses to tell Harry to go back. He just lays the facts before them, and leaves the ultimate choice up to them.

This is a perfect bookend to the Potter series: a choice presented to Lily/Harry, a choice made to protect their loved ones, and the resulting magic leading to Voldemort's undoing. Dumbledore placed his faith in the power of Lily's choice before, and now he does the same for Harry's choice, after spending five years stressing the importance of choices to the boy.

Dumbledore's faith—and his earlier teachings—prove well-founded, as Harry does indeed make the right choice.

So at least that part went as Dumbledore intended . . . unlike most of his plans.

When Plans Go Wrong

Most of the plans I have listed here did go horribly wrong at some point or other, but none more so than the last one. Dumbledore's Plan D hinged on Harry becoming master of the Hallows. Cloak? Check. Stone? Check. Elder Wand? About that. . .

Harry explains it all to Voldemort, and to us, at the climax of the series.

> "The Elder Wand recognized a new master before Dumbledore died, someone who never even laid a hand on it. The new master removed the wand from Dumbledore against his will, never realizing exactly what he had done, or that the world's most dangerous wand had given him its allegiance. . . ."
>
> [. . .]
>
> "The true master of the Elder Wand was Draco Malfoy."
>
> [. . .]
>
> "I [Harry] overpowered Draco weeks ago. I took this wand from him."
>
> [. . .]
>
> "I am the true master of the Elder Wand." (DH742-743)

Dumbledore's elaborate plan for Harry to master the Hallows falls apart moments before Dumbledore actually dies, when Draco Disarms Dumbledore and becomes the master of the Elder Wand. This is the flaw in the plan that lends itself to the chapter's title. It means that Snape is not the Elder Wand's master, which means that Harry will not become the wand's master by defeating Snape. Plan D should be scrapped at this point.[68]

It's also worth noting the reason Plan D goes so awry: Dumbledore takes the few valuable seconds he has, and instead defending himself against Draco's Disarming Spell, uses that time to immobilize Harry for Harry's own protection. This is a microcosm of everything Dumbledore has done: completely disregard his previously established plans, all to take care of Harry. In the middle of *Deathly Hallows*, there is a heartbreaking line: "[Harry] closed his eyes at [Hermione's] touch, and hated himself for wishing that what she said was true: that Dumbledore had really cared." (DH362) If only Harry knew just how much Dumbledore cared!

So, in fact, the line that foreshadowed Dumbledore's Machiavellian tendencies at the beginning of *Deathly Hallows* is misdirection on multiple levels. Elphias Doge wrote in his obituary of Dumbledore that "He died as he lived: working always for the greater good." (DH20) That is actually untrue in both interpretations of "for the greater good," the sweet interpretation as the common good, and the sinister interpretation of Machiavellianism. Because when Dumbledore died, he was not working for the greater good: his last act was to protect Harry.

---

[68] Ironically enough, this is the second time Dumbledore's carefully laid plans have been foiled by a Malfoy. These instances occur in Books 2 and 6, which intentionally mirror each other.

As soon as Dumbledore is killed, someone needs to put the kibosh on Plan D because Draco is the master of the Elder Wand. However, it's far too late to do anything about it! The book and Snitch were already bequeathed to Hermione and Harry, respectively—Dumbledore's portrait can't exactly snatch them back from the Ministry. Since Harry never comes to talk with the portrait or Snape, there is no opportunity to tell him that the Hallows quest is folly. Harry somehow mastering the wand by defeating Draco is almost completely out of the realm of possibility, since they certainly won't be dueling anytime soon, and it would be silly to attempt facilitating such an event.

So Harry continues pursuing the Hallows (which at least accomplishes one of Dumbledore's goals—delaying Harry's death). Even worse, Snape is now a target for Voldemort, and neither he nor Harry receive any actual benefit from that. "Poor Severus" (DH721) indeed!

But luck and happenstance succeed where Dumbledore's plans failed. Through a series of unforeseen events, Harry ends up a prisoner at Malfoy Manor during the week that Draco is home for the holidays, putting them in a perfect position for a face-off. And in a blink-and-you-miss-it moment, Dumbledore's last plan gets back on track: "Harry took his chance: He leapt over an armchair and wrested the three wands from Draco's grip" (DH474). This action is not even deigned its own sentence, yet it changes everything, because Harry defeats Draco and masters the Elder Wand by doing so.

To be clear, I do not think that Dumbledore ever planned for what happened in the final duel between Harry and Voldemort: that Voldemort, in possession of the Elder Wand, would have a Killing Curse rebound because Harry was its true master. There is no mention in the books, amidst all the discussion about mastering the wand, that indicates Dumbledore planned for Voldemort to actually own the wand. He knew that Voldemort would be searching for the wand, but he did not expect Voldemort to succeed. I think Dumbledore expected Snape to be able to keep the wand from Voldemort, trusting to Snape's own prodigious skill and cunning to outfox Voldemort—Snape probably had instructions to go into the tomb and snag the wand if Voldemort got close. However, Voldemort's quest for the Elder Wand was done much more on the down-low than his quests usually are, so Snape was unaware of the need to intervene until it was too late.

Putting Plans in Their Place

"But, no, I really wanted, very consciously, for the history of the wizarding world to hinge on this moment where two teenage boys have a physical [fight]. They don't even do it by magic.

"That sort of puts all of Voldemort's and Dumbledore's grandiose plans in their place, doesn't it? You just can't plan that well, that something can go wrong and it went wrong . . . It went wrong because Harry managed to pull this wand out of Draco's grip."[69]

It must be said, this is one of my favorite quotes of Jo's from any of her interviews. It really puts things in perspective, doesn't it? Dumbledore had so many carefully laid plans before he died. He planned for eventualities and had backups, and then in the end, most of his plans ended up completely useless.

Plan D (making Harry the master of Death) worked through a lot of coincidences, after being

---

[69] Meredith Vieira, "TODAY interview with J.K. Rowling," July 30, 2007, http://today.msnbc.msn.com/id/20035573/ns/today-wild_about_harry/t/confused-potter-author-sets-record-straight/#.T-qgbbWe4xA.

rendered obsolete by Draco Disarming Dumbledore. But it wasn't needed, because Voldemort tethering Harry to life ended up being enough.

Plan C (delaying the moment Harry finds out he has to die) very nearly failed for several reasons, chief among them that Voldemort succeeded in finding the Elder Wand and killed Snape just as it was unfolding.

Plan B (Snape defeating Voldemort should Harry die) never had the chance to come to pass on account of Harry living and Snape dying. Snape could not have defeated Voldemort, because he predeceased Harry, but someone else probably would have after receiving protection from Harry's sacrifice.

And the only plan that did end up working as designed was Plan A—destroying Horcruxes, Harry sacrificing himself and coming back to life in order to defeat Voldemort. Sometimes, the most straightforward plan is the most effective. Harry also got the bonus of not having to actually kill Voldemort, but that wasn't part of the plan.

Since I can only imagine how much your head must be spinning by now (since I know mine is), at the end of the chapter is a handy diagram of all of Dumbledore's plans for what will happen after he dies. As you can see, there are two key moments: Harry finding out he has to die, and the actual sacrifice.

Worth noting is that all of Dumbledore's plans for the entire wizarding world focused on only two individuals that we know of: Harry and Snape. Dumbledore treats all his other allies as pawns and only Harry and Snape as significant chess pieces. But the focus on Harry was at Snape's expense. Dumbledore concentrated all his efforts on keeping Harry alive, whereas he trusted Snape to stay alive through his own formidable intelligence. And for all that went wrong, in the end Dumbledore achieved his two objectives: defeating Voldemort and saving Harry.

THE LIFE AND LIES OF ALBUS DUMBLEDORE 169

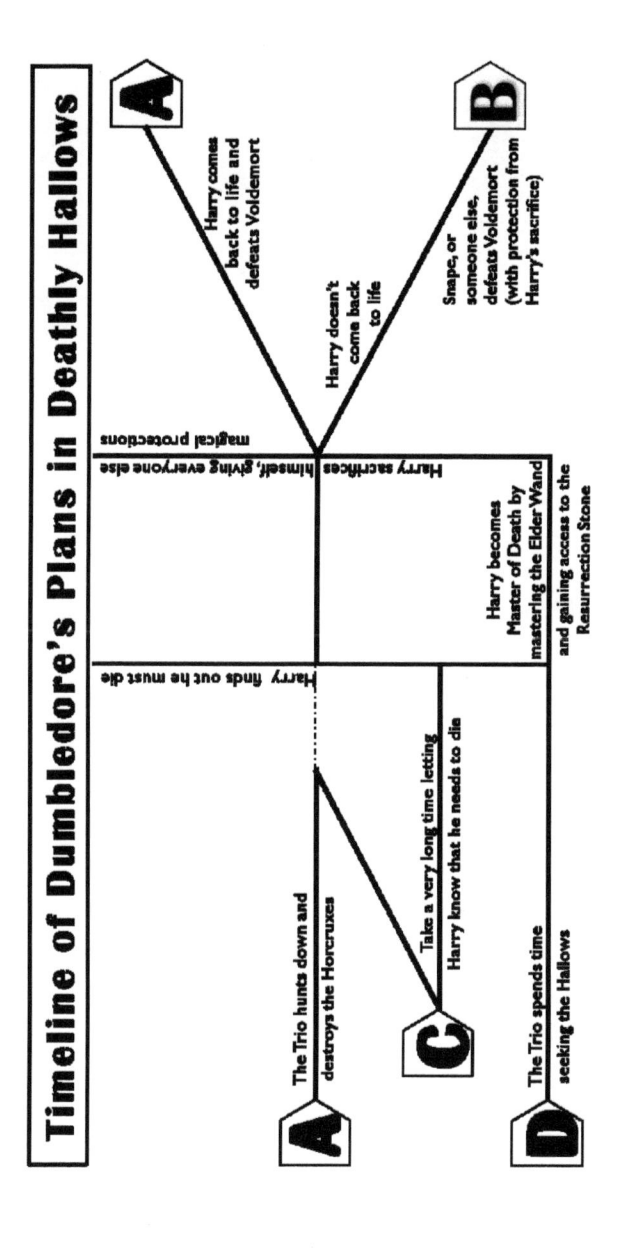

Timeline of Dumbledore's Plans in Deathly Hallows

A. The Trio hunts down and destroys the Horcruxes

D. The Trio spends time seeking the Hallows

C. Take a very long time letting Harry know that he needs to die

Harry finds out he must die

Harry becomes Master of Death by mastering the Elder Wand and gaining access to the Resurrection Stone

Harry sacrifices himself, giving everyone else magical protections

A. Harry comes back to life and defeats Voldemort

B. Snape, or someone else, defeats Voldemort (with protection from Harry's sacrifice)

Harry doesn't come back to life

Chapter 7:
Albus Dumbledore and the Deathly Hallows

> *"But there were any number of things that would seem incredible about Dumbledore; that he had once received bottom marks in a Transfiguration test, for instance, or had taken up goat-charming like Aberforth...." (DH182)*

So wonders Harry in *Deathly Hallows* upon reading a truncated letter of his mother's. But perhaps the most incredible thing about Dumbledore is that, although he's dead in *Deathly Hallows*, the character looms larger than ever before, because of the surprising and fascinating focus on his legacy that pervades the book.

This is very appropriate given that Dumbledore is Machiavelli's Prince, and much of his strategy relied on maintaining a sterling reputation. Because as soon as Dumbledore is no longer around to defend himself, everyone has an awful lot to say about him.

Before the word "Horcruxes" is even brought up in the seventh book—by page 28—we have read two wildly contradictory stories about Dumbledore: Elphias Doge's and Rita Skeeter's. Even as the wizarding world crumbles around him, Harry becomes consumed trying to parse out which version is closer to the truth.

We begin with perhaps the most rose-tinted version of Dumbledore, as his childhood best friend eulogizes him in the *Daily Prophet* (DH16-20). But no one sets very much store by what Doge says, because he "skated over the sticky patches in that obituary of yours!" (DH153) Rita Skeeter's aspersions on his intelligence are expected, but Auntie Muriel also says, "Oh, we all know you worshipped Dumbledore!" (DH154) Aberforth gets the final word, and he (very colorfully) concurs: Elphias "thought the sun shone out of my brother's every orifice." (DH563)

Of course, the other sources provided aren't reliable either. We already know not to trust Rita Skeeter, even before Elphias Doge says that "Skeeter's book contains less fact than a Chocolate Frog card." (DH24) As Hermione astutely points out, "Harry, do you really think you'll get the truth from a malicious old woman like Muriel, or from Rita Skeeter?" (DH185) So we have to wade through a lot of misinformation before getting to the truth from the Dumbledore brothers.

There are two key aspects of Dumbledore's past that are brought into question: his family history and his brief youthful flirtation with the Dark Arts and wizard supremacy.

The Dumbledore Family

Most of what happened to the Dumbledores boils down to the question of who Ariana was and how she died. Theories and rumors run rampant through the last book, and the tragedy of what happened to her reverberates through everything else that happened: Percival's incarceration, Kendra's death, the falling out between Albus and Grindelwald, and the rift between Albus and Aberforth.

Everyone Harry speaks to has their own guess or opinion. Elphias Doge feebly sticks to the party line: "Ariana was delicate!" (DH155) Muriel guesses that Albus "did away with his Squib sister!" (DH154) And Rita Skeeter puts a sinister spin on the whole thing:

> Was she the inadvertent victim of some Dark rite? Did she stumble across something she ought not to have done, as the two young men sat practicing for their attempt at glory and domination? Is it possible that Ariana Dumbledore was the first person to die "for the greater good"? (DH359)

The truth can only come from a primary source: Aberforth Dumbledore, who reveals the full tragedy of the Dumbledore family to the Trio right before the Battle of Hogwarts. (The story is then corroborated by Albus Dumbledore at King's Cross, so we know it to be factual.) The story is awful: Ariana was traumatized by Muggle boys; Percival incarcerated for seeking retribution; Kendra killed accidentally by her unstable daughter; "And Ariana . . . after all my mother's care and caution . . . lay dead upon the floor" due to a stray spell in a duel among Albus, Aberforth, and Grindelwald (DH717). But the story is also reassuring in that nothing evil was being done by the Dumbledores—they were all handling a bad situation as best they could.

"He Was Young"

Far more interesting to consider is that Dumbledore was, indeed, culpable of making some very bad decisions in his youth: plotting with Grindelwald to subjugate Muggles. Harry and Hermione very clearly delineate the two opposing arguments here.

Harry responds emotionally and will not excuse Dumbledore because of his youth.

> "I thought you'd say 'They were young.' They were the same age as we are now. And here we are, risking our lives to fight the Dark Arts, and there he was, in a huddle with his new best friend, plotting their rise to power over the Muggles." (DH361)[70]

Hermione, on the other hand, adopts a more lenient stance.

> "He changed, Harry, he changed! It's as simple as that! Maybe he did believe these things when he was seventeen, but the whole of the rest of his life was devoted to fighting the Dark Arts! Dumbledore was the one who stopped Grindelwald, the one who always voted for Muggle protection and Muggle-born rights, who fought You-Know-Who from the start, and who died trying to bring him down!" (DH361)

The fascinating thing is that both arguments, which are both valid, received some of their strongest backup from none other than Albus Dumbledore himself.

---

[70] As an aside, it's hard to express how much this passage meant to me when I read it as a teenager. In a world that seemed wholly dismissive of anyone under eighteen, this was exactly what I needed. It was so empowering to read about teenagers not only doing awesome things, but also being held accountable for their actions. Because holding people accountable for their actions in their youth implies that teenagers are sentient beings capable of making decisions, which flew in the face of literally everything everyone did in the real world.

The chief reason that Harry's argument holds water is how he makes it from the moral high ground: he is doing things no teenager should have to do. Of course, it's not Dumbledore's fault that Voldemort regained corporeal form much sooner than preferred and was facing off against a teen Harry instead of a hardened middle-aged Auror Harry. But it's still Dumbledore's deployment of his young protégés that casts his own youthful mistakes in such an unflattering light.

But to Hermione's point, Dumbledore is renowned as someone who "believes in second chances." (GF472) For example, he offers one to Severus Snape and to Draco Malfoy, both Death Eaters. Now we know why he's so adamant about that: he himself needed a second chance at age eighteen. He knows what it's like to have your actions lead to unthinkable deadly consequences, so he shows mercy to those who've gone through a similar ordeal.

Dumbledore's Army

Perhaps the most powerful statement about Dumbledore's legacy is one that flies under the radar: the DA. Even after all the slander Dumbledore was subject to during that year, it is "Dumbledore's Army, Still Recruiting!" (DH575) Elphias Doge makes the bold claim that Dumbledore "was the most inspiring and the best loved of all Hogwarts headmasters." (DH20) And though we know that to not be true for a quarter of the wizarding population—those who wear emerald and silver—it appears to be true for the three houses present in the Room of Requirement.

What makes this so impactful is that there is an alternative readily available: Potter's Army. Recall that Dumbledore invested a lot of energy in turning Harry into a symbol; the Order rallies around him and Hagrid throws "Support Harry Potter" parties (DH442). But the DA, who may have even more belief in Harry than a laywizard who wasn't taught D.A.D.A. by him, chooses to remain affiliated with Dumbledore.

On the one hand, there are practical reasons for this: the legacy of the original DA, and the association of Dumbledore to Hogwarts. Dumbledore and the school have been intricately entwined in the Wizarding public's consciousness for a long time. The reason Hogwarts was always a bastion against Voldemort was because Dumbledore was there. Dumbledore was the Headmaster for two entire generations of wizards, for forty-one years. Dumbledore was even buried on school grounds, in an unprecedented move, never to be separated from the school.

The first time the DA formed, it was to defend Hogwarts against an evil regime that had ousted Dumbledore. That mission statement is no different this time around, so there is no reason to change the name.

But we must also consider who made the decision to keep the name. We are told that the leadership of the group fell to Neville, Luna, and Ginny. Assuming Luna can't be bothered with such mundane things as group names (Snorkack Army, anyone?), it would have been Neville and Ginny making the call, whether or not they had input from the rest of the DA. It so happens that Neville and Ginny are uniquely suited to believe the best of Dumbledore.

Neville has grown up with his formidable grandmother, who always stood by Dumbledore ("[Augusta] says it's the *Daily Prophet* that's going downhill, not Dumbledore. [...] She says if Dumbledore says he's back, he's back." OP219). Judging by his reaction in the Department of Mysteries ("'Dubbledore!' said Neville, his sweaty face suddenly transported" OP805), Dumbledore meant a lot to him. His Gran would no doubt dismiss all of Rita Skeeter's lies out of hand. But Neville is also someone who has changed a lot from his youth. It would not seem so outlandish to him that Dumbledore could have changed as well.

And then there's Ginny, who would identify with a young Dumbledore more than most. Recall that she too, in her youth, was seduced by a charismatic Dark wizard. She, too, was party to atrocities committed by said Dark wizard; she was just lucky that no one died. And when the truth was revealed, when she was sure she would be expelled, Dumbledore showed mercy. He comforted her, forgave her, and gave her a second chance to turn into the formidable witch she became. If he gave her a second chance, why should she begrudge him one?

In Doge's obituary, he says Dumbledore was "to his last hour, as willing to stretch out a hand to a small boy with dragon pox as he was on the day that I met him." (DH20) On the one hand, we know that was not necessarily always true. Dumbledore was remote from his students, and he rarely extended a hand to Slytherins. However, when he didn't have to make choices affecting the entire wizarding world, and when Slytherins weren't involved, he was kind and caring. He showed mercy to a young Ginny, he delicately protected Neville. And now he is rewarded by the faith of his former students; the name "Dumbledore's Army" will prove to be a much more enduring legacy than Rita Skeeter's book.

And the students' loyalty is rewarded by Hogwarts itself, which creates a passage from the Room of Requirement to Aberforth's quarters above the Hog's Head. On the surface, this is purely to satisfy the students' need for food. But it could be that the Room of Requirement anticipated what Aberforth needed— to regain hope—and multitasked by creating the passage specifically to his bar.

It's very notable how exactly this passage works: it is hidden behind a portrait of Ariana Dumbledore, who goes to fetch Neville when the Trio shows up. It's kind of perfect that Dumbledore's Army will go through a Dumbledore (a DumbleDOOR, if you will) to a Dumbledore; and a Dumbledore will keep Dumbledore's Army thriving.

This is a masterclass in symbolism: Ariana Dumbledore serves as the go-between for Aberforth Dumbledore and [Albus] Dumbledore's Army. Her death tore the brothers apart; her memory is what brings them together.

Password?

> Harry ran without stopping, clutching the crystal flask of Snape's last thoughts, and he did not slow down until he reached the stone gargoyle guarding the headmaster's office.
>
> "Password?"
>
> "Dumbledore!" said Harry without thinking, because it was he whom he yearned to see, and to his surprise the gargoyle slid aside, revealing the spiral staircase behind. (DH662)

There are two potential explanations for the password being "Dumbledore," and both are a powerful statement about Dumbledore's legacy.

The first, recently espoused by Lorrie Kim,[71] is that this password was chosen deliberately by Snape to honor Dumbledore. This is a nice sentiment, and is

---

[71] https://lorriekimcom.wordpress.com/2018/10/20/and-my-soul-dumbledore-the-snape-dumbledore-relationship/
"During his year as headmaster, the unguessable word that guarded Snape's space was a name that kept him as safe as any Fidelius Charm."

certainly possible. That said, it seems too high a risk for Snape to take as a purely symbolic gesture. The password to the headmaster's office has to be something that can be revealed to people—students and faculty—who may need to meet with the headmaster. Obviously, having the password be "Dumbledore" won't work if the Carrows have a question for Headmaster Snape.

So the implication is that Snape created a second secret password, "Dumbledore," pretty much solely for sentimental reasons. This seems most unlike Snape: the risk is too high that someone would shout "Dumbledore" outside his office, and the payoff of such a symbolic gesture is too small.

Far more likely, in my opinion, is that it is the stone gargoyle that accepted Dumbledore's name as a password. We know that parts of Hogwarts have some sentience: the Room of Requirement (as mentioned earlier), and the front doors (whom Flitwick teaches to recognize Sirius Black, PA269). I think the gargoyle, who has been guarding Dumbledore's office for forty years,[72] grew quite fond of Dumbledore.

As an aside, we don't know whether it was the gargoyle or Dumbledore himself who was responsible for frustrating Umbridge in OotP: "Couldn't get past the gargoyle. The Head's office has sealed itself against her." (OP625) On the one hand, it would be in character for the gargoyle to keep Umbridge out if it really is that appreciative of Dumbledore. On the other hand, it was also be in character for Dumbledore himself to seal the Head's office against Umbridge to spite her. Either explanation makes me happy.

But back to *Deathly Hallows*: the fact that the gargoyle accepts "Dumbledore!" as an override of its

---

[72] We know the gargoyle has guarded the Head's office since at least Dippet's time at Hogwarts, because Tom Riddle passes the gargoyle the night he frames Hagrid. (CS245)

security protocols speaks to Dumbledore's legacy in the eyes of Hogwarts itself. In the Battle of Hogwarts, Dumbledore's Army is a crucial part of the "Hogwartians." And like its defenders, Hogwarts has immense respect for Dumbledore when all is said and done.

Epilogue:
Judging Dumbledore

"Well, of course, Dumbledore is a biographer's dream," Rita Skeeter says (DH23), and indeed he has been. We have now reached the end of the series, and there are several takeaways from viewing the Harry Potter books through this lens. Dumbledore is not omniscient—every instance where he seems to be, we can explain his reasoning in the moment. Dumbledore likes being in control and uses his knowledge of Lord Voldemort to manipulate his foe. Dumbledore is usually meticulous, thinking through the details and planning things years in advance. There is always some bigger picture going on just off the pages of the books, usually involving Dumbledore being impressive and Jo being even more impressive. The biggest takeaway of all: almost everything Dumbledore did was for Harry.

Make no mistake: Dumbledore was Machiavellian. He did what he believed needed to be done in order to defeat Voldemort. He fought for the greater good. In the course of this battle, he behaved ruthlessly. He was incredibly cruel to Snape, and when necessary, he did plan Harry's death. Rita Skeeter calls the relationship between Harry and Dumbledore "unhealthy, even sinister." (DH27)

But Dumbledore's Machiavellian tendencies did have a limit, and that limit was Harry. The sensible and utilitarian thing to do would have been to allow Harry to sacrifice himself, to die if need be, in order for Voldemort to be defeated. And although Dumbledore knew that must happen eventually, he struggled against it in every way he could. He procrastinated, he delayed things, he set up schemes to give Harry a better chance of survival. And luckily for all involved, Harry did indeed survive.

Evaluating the morality of Dumbledore's actions, now that they're clear, will have to be undertaken by every reader individually. I look forward to debating it, but I will leave you with a verdict from three parties that are very invested in Albus Dumbledore.

First and foremost, J.K. Rowling. In 2008, Jo did an interview with Adeel Amini, where she had this to say about her newly controversial headmaster: "He's an innately good man."[73]

Second, Harry Potter. Of those still alive, he has perhaps suffered the most due to Dumbledore. And in many ways, his relationship with the headmaster mirrored the fandom's perception of Dumbledore: we spent our formative years believing him to be a paragon of virtue, but after *Deathly Hallows*, we were filled with anger and a sense of betrayal. For Harry, the turning point was the chapter "King's Cross," where Harry acknowledged the awful things Dumbledore did, yet forgave him.

Harry's verdict on Dumbledore comes to us in the Epilogue (DH753). He has named his son Albus. Not Sirius, who's relegated to a middle name. Not Remus, who makes no appearance in Harry's brood. *Albus*. There can be no higher token of Harry's esteem.

Finally, I offer my own verdict, because I now know where I stand on Dumbledore's morality.

The practical (more Ravenclaw) side of me is appalled by Dumbledore's dangerous sentimentality. Dumbledore let people die, he gambled the entire future of the wizarding world on keeping one boy alive and happy just a little bit longer. Thinking about it

---

[73] https://medium.com/@adeelamini/the-adeel-amini-jk-rowling-interview-a05a62071458

logically, this is horrible and I should hate Dumbledore all the more for it.

But I can't bring myself to hate Dumbledore now, because this just proves his love for Harry. The fact that Dumbledore loved Harry so much, that he was willing to risk everything because he cared about Harry, is something worth admiring in my opinion. It shows that Dumbledore is human after all and exemplifies the virtues of love that he always extolled.

Much like Harry, all I wanted in *Deathly Hallows* was proof that Dumbledore actually cared about something other than his greater good—that there was some shred left of the benevolent wizard we thought we knew in the first six books. So after many confusing years trying to puzzle it out, crafting this book has been like my own King's Cross, as I hope reading it may be for even a few of you. Once I lay Dumbledore's cards on the table, stripped of salacious gossip and unfounded assumptions, I could acknowledge his faults and forgive them—returning to love Dumbledore almost as much as when I first wept for him in *Half-Blood Prince*.

> "In other words, I acted exactly as Voldemort expects we fools who love to act."
> —Albus Dumbledore (OP838)

Appendix A:
The Timeline

Figuring out dates in Harry Potter can seem a touch futile, since Rowling has often confessed she's no great shakes at math. However, certain timelines are significant enough for her to have paid attention; among those is Voldemort's. The timeline of who's Headmaster of Hogwarts factors into this significantly, so it appears Rowling was detailed enough for us to craft a timeline.

Most importantly, we should figure out when Dumbledore became Headmaster. Through several clues, we can pinpoint the start of his tenure at December 1956. McGonagall says that she will have been teaching Transfiguration for "Thirty-nine years this December," (OP321) in 1995. So she started teaching in December 1956. This doubtlessly coincided with Dumbledore, the previous Transfiguration teacher, leaving the post, presumably by becoming Headmaster.

This fits in with the time-table around Voldemort's visit to Hogwarts to ask for the D.A.D.A. position. In the flashback, Voldemort says, "I heard that you had become headmaster," (HBP441), indicating this was a recent appointment. We are told that this is "ten years" after Tom Riddle murdered Hepzibah Smith (HBP440). Tom Riddle graduated Hogwarts in summer of 1945, so if we assume he worked at Borgin and Burkes for a year or so, that would place this visit in the winter of 1956-1957, just after Dumbledore became Headmaster.

As an aside: that means that Voldemort spent about fourteen years consolidating his power after making his fifth Horcrux (the diadem) and hiding it at Hogwarts, before fully unleashing his reign of terror. When he falls in October 1981, Dumbledore says, "We've had precious little to celebrate for eleven years." So Voldemort was wreaking havoc from 1970 onwards.

Back to the headmasters. We know that Armando Dippet was Dumbledore's immediate predecessor. Since he was at Hogwarts during Riddle's tenure, he was Headmaster from at least the mid-1930s onwards. However, we also know that he put Professor Kettleburn on probation sixty-two times (TBB39). Let us assume that Dippet put Kettleburn on probation twice a year on average (which is still quite impressive!). That would give Dippet a tenure as Headmaster of 31 years, meaning he would have become Headmaster in 1925. Of course, it could have been quite a bit earlier, since Dippet is portrayed as very old, but we can be reasonably sure he started no later than the mid-1920s.

We can go back further, and ask who was Armando Dippet's predecessor? All signs point to it being Phineas Nigellus Black. Phineas Nigellus's dates from the Black Family Tree fit perfectly. His date of death is given as 1925—which is exactly the year we've deduced Dippet became Headmaster! That seems like no coincidence. Moreover, if Phineas was born in 1847, he would likely be the Headmaster preceding Dippet; otherwise, he would have been a very young Headmaster.[74]

---

[74] If one wants to consider Pottermore, we can go back even further, and have a potential candidate for Phineas Nigellus's predecessor. In the Pottermore entry for Peeves, we get mention of Eupraxia Mole being Headmistress in 1876. Phineas can't have been before her (he'd only be thirty-one

We can now create a thorough list of the Heads in the twentieth century:

> Late 19th/early 20th century—1925: Phineas Nigellus Black
> 1925—1956: Armando Dippet
> 1956—1997: Albus Dumbledore
> 1996: Dolores Umbridge (Disputed)
> 1997—1998: Severus Snape
> 1998—present: Minerva McGonagall

The other question that often comes up is when Dumbledore was born. Different apocryphal sources give different answers, while the published books are silent on the matter, which indicates Rowling never thought it was relevant enough to think through. So we'll leave that one well enough alone.

---

in 1876), so he was Headmaster after her, and possibly directly after.

Appendix B:
Dumbledore's Most Puzzling Lie

I keep having issues with Dumbledore's conversation with Harry at the end of *Sorcerer's Stone*. Dumbledore promises, "I shall answer your questions unless I have a very good reason not to, in which case I beg you'll forgive me. I shall not, of course, lie." (SS298)

He then proceeds to not only omit quite a few relevant details, but does tell an outright lie: "[Y]our father did something Snape could never forgive. [...] He saved his life. [...] Professor Snape couldn't bear being in your father's debt.... I do believe he worked so hard to protect you this year because he felt that would make him and your father even. Then he could go back to hating your father's memory in peace...." (SS300)

While Snape's true motivation obviously was not Dumbledore's secret to tell, this whopper seems like a singularly bad idea. It abated Harry's curiosity for two years, but the truth eventually surfaced and it was not pleasant for anybody.

This was also rather inconsistent with Dumbledore's modus operandi, which was to tell half-truths or simply withhold information. Especially considering Dumbledore just set a precedent for withholding information, regarding Voldemort's motivation for attacking Harry, he could have just said, "No comment. Next question."

The only theory I have come across is Theowyn's, in their essay that shares a title with this book (it really is a good title!).[75] Theowyn claims that Dumbledore told this lie to encourage the animosity between Snape and Harry, as their antagonism gave Dumbledore more control over both of them. I don't buy that, because Theowyn's reading of Dumbledore is incredibly sinister; in fact, it's probably the harshest analysis of Dumbledore that I've read.

However, I'm at a loss to offer an alternative theory. I leave this to you, dear reader, and beg you to let me know of anything you come up with.

---

[75] http://www.the-leaky-cauldron.org/features/essays/issue21/lifeandliesalbusdumbledore/

Appendix C:
Dumbledore as Death

Many years after *Deathly Hallows* was released, when it seemed the fandom was slowing down, a new theory began making the rounds, eventually reaching the pinnacle for fan theories: Jo Rowling's Twitter. When a fan named Abbie Owen-Jones asked Jo what her favorite theory was in 2015, Jo replied, "Dumbledore as death. It's a beautiful theory and it fits."[76]

Spearheading the discussion about this theory since then is Andrew Sims, who laid it out beautifully in an article on Hypable,[77] and has since discussed it on MuggleCast #358.[78] I would be remiss not to include this theory in a book about Dumbledore, so here is a breakdown.

The theory posits that The Tale of Three Brothers is a parallel to the events of the Harry Potter series. The trio that Harry once termed "the abandoned boys" (DH697) represent the three brothers of the tale; with Dumbledore serving as Death. Whether deliberate or not on Jo's part, there is a beautiful symmetry here.

---

[76] https://twitter.com/jk_rowling/status/634666937990152192?lang=en
[77] https://www.hypable.com/dumbledore-death-theory/
[78] http://mugglecast.com/episode-358-dumbledore-snape-harry-three-brothers/
Also worth reading are the comments on MuggleCast's Patreon, https://www.patreon.com/posts/patreon-question-17448172 .

The Three Brothers

Voldemort represents the oldest brother, Antioch Peverell, who received the Elder Wand from Death. "So the oldest brother, who was a combative man, asked for a wand more powerful than any in existence: a wand that must always win duels for its owner, a wand worthy of a wizard who had conquered Death!" (DH407) Crucially, Voldemort actually uses that exact turn of phrase when he is resurrected: "You know my goal—to conquer death." (GF653) Like the oldest brother, Voldemort is a combative man seeking the most powerful wand.

> "The first brother [. . .] sought out a fellow wizard with whom he had a quarrel. Naturally, with the Elder Wand as his weapon, he could not fail to win the duel that followed. Leaving his enemy dead upon the floor, the oldest brother proceeded to an inn, where he boasted loudly of the powerful wand he had snatched from Death himself, and of how it made him invincible." (DH408)

Voldemort, too, seeks out the wizard with whom he has a quarrel: Harry. He leaves Harry dead on the floor at first, then returns to Hogwarts, boasting loudly of how he triumphed over Harry Potter. But his arrogance proves his undoing, as (like Antioch) he is killed that very night.

Severus Snape represents the middle brother, Cadmus Peverell, who received the Resurrection Stone from Death. The key similarity here is a shared longing for a long-lost love. When Cadmus uses the Stone, "the figure of the girl he had once hoped to marry, before her untimely death, appeared at once before him."

(DH409) Snape, too, is consumed with longing for a girl he loved before her untimely death: Lily Evans.

Harry Potter represents the youngest brother, Ignotus Peverell, who received the Invisibility Cloak from Death. "The youngest brother was the humblest and also the wisest of the brothers" (DH408)—as Harry certainly is of the abandoned boys. And like Ignotus, Harry is the only one of the three to evade death—living a long, full life, with sons that he doubtless bequeathed the Cloak to one day.

Death

That's well and good, but where does Dumbledore come in?

Like Death, Dumbledore was instrumental in distributing the Hallows to the brothers. Voldemort literally took the Elder Wand out of Dumbledore's dead hands. And like Death, Dumbledore gave the Invisibility Cloak to Harry in *Sorcerer's Stone*. But the interesting one is Snape, who never received the Resurrection Stone. Dumbledore may not have given him the Stone, but he replicated its effects for Snape. When he charged Snape with protecting Harry, he provided Snape with a poor imitation of the woman he loved: her son, who may have her eyes and her "deepest nature," (DH684) but looks mostly like Snape's enemy.

We are given another subtle clue by the fact that Voldemort fears death above all else.[79] And ever since the first book, everyone keeps saying that "Dumbledore was the only wizard Voldemort had ever

---

[79] This is said obliquely several times in the text, usually by Dumbledore, and Jo spelled it out in her 2005 interview with Melissa Anelli and Emerson Spartz: "His worst fear is death." http://www.accio-quote.org/articles/2005/0705-tlc_mugglenet-anelli-2.htm

feared." This is said by Hermione (SS260), Bill Weasley (OP92), twice by Harry (GF679/HBP72), and it even lends itself to the title of *Order of the Phoenix* chapter 36. The conflation of Dumbledore with Death renders these statements doubly true: Dumbledore is the only one Voldemort ever feared because he is Death, and Voldemort's worst fear is death.

Dumbledore was also the key orchestrator of the deaths of each of the abandoned boys. He devoted all the last years of his life to destroying Voldemort, and in the end, his plan succeeded. As we discussed in Chapter 6, Dumbledore painted a target on Snape's back by asking Snape to kill him; Snape's death at Voldemort's hands can be attributed to Dumbledore. And Dumbledore's final master plan revolved around Harry laying down his life, which Harry did because of what Dumbledore said in The Prince's Tale.

But note the difference: where Snape and especially Voldemort greeted death unwillingly, Harry made the choice to sacrifice his life. "The youngest brother finally took off the Cloak of Invisibility and gave it to his son. And then he greeted Death as an old friend." (DH409) Right before Harry is hit by the Killing Curse, he "pulled off the Invisibility Cloak." (DH703) And then Harry greets Dumbledore as an old friend in King's Cross.

The theory is incredibly elegant, and it fits the text very well. It's incredibly exciting that new Potter scholarship like this is still being developed and will continue to be for many years to come. So in light of this, I thank you for reading a book all about Death. Let us go together gladly, and, equals, continue the discussion about Albus Percival Wulfric Brian Dumbledore.

Bibliography

As I said in my introduction, this book is built upon the foundation of all the Harry Potter essays I read over the course of fifteen years of fandom. I owe a huge debt of gratitude to the writers who put their cleverness into the essays at The Lexicon, The Leaky Cauldron, and mighty MuggleNet. Throughout my teenage years, I read all the essays posted on those websites voraciously—naturally, I wish I'd kept better track of the stuff I read. But these are the best pieces I could recall about Albus Dumbledore, and I highly recommend reading all of them to anyone interested in further examining this fascinating character.

Also, anyone looking for a comprehensive fictional biography of Albus Dumbledore would do well to visit his page on *The Harry Potter Lexicon*: https://www.hp-lexicon.org/character/dumbledore-family/albus-dumbledore/. The page is useful for both fast facts and for insightful analysis (like the etymology of his name, for example).

This book was always meant to generate further conversation, and I'm thrilled to say that it already has. Lorrie Kim wrote an insightful series of chapter-by-chapter responses to this book's first edition on her blog! https://lorriekimcom.wordpress.com/2018/10

A note about the hyperlinks: MuggleNet, where most of these essays are hosted, has a habit of redesigning itself every few years and breaking all of its links. So if the page is not found, simply put the author and title into Google, and that will pull it up. If any other links go wonky, input them into the Wayback Machine (web.archive.org) with a pre-2017 date.

Post-*Deathly Hallows* Era

Josie Kearns; "Philosopher's Stone—Dumbledore's Perspective"
https://hp-companion.com/ps/psessay
    Josie Kearns is one of the foremost essayists of the post-*Deathly Hallows* era, and her entire website (hp-companion.com) is worth reading through for analysis of the seven books. I tend to agree with her on a lot of what Dumbledore was scheming. However, she tends to credit the characters with knowing, deducing, and orchestrating much more than I do. In her essay on *Sorcerer's Stone*, she reaches the same end goal I do for Dumbledore but theorizes that Dumbledore knew Quirrell was possessed from the get-go and set traps accordingly.

Josie Kearns; "What Did Dobby Know?"
https://hp-companion.com/essays/csessay
    This essay does not pertain to Dumbledore per se, but it does explain what Lucius was up to during *Chamber of Secrets*, which helps us understand why that tripped Dumbledore up.

Josie Kearns; "Needing More Time"
https://hp-companion.com/essays/paessay/
    Josie's perspective on the climax of *Prisoner of Azkaban* is that Dumbledore pretty much knew everything going on the entire time.

Josie Kearns; "A Very Bad Year for Albus Dumbledore (and it's all Snape's fault)"
https://hp-companion.com/essays/gfessay
    Probably my favorite HP essay, this lays out why Dumbledore is at a loss during *Goblet of Fire*. It illustrates how the breakdown in communication between Snape and Dumbledore was instrumental in

allowing Crouch Jr. to get away with masquerading as Moody.

Josie Kearns; "Harry Potter, Occlumens?"
https://hp-companion.com/essays/opessay/
　　Josie lays out an intriguing theory that Dumbledore set up the Occlumency lessons to fail on purpose.

Josie Kearns; "Prophecy"
https://hp-companion.com/essays/prophecy/
　　This essay discusses the Ministry's knowledge of the prophecy, which puts their interactions with Harry and Dumbledore in a fascinating new light.

mirrormere; "The Flaw in the Plan"
http://www.mugglenet.com/2011/01/the-flaw-in-the-plan/
　　This essay is very similar to what you just read in this book but uses a similar style of deep dive into the books to reach nearly the opposite conclusions I did: namely, that Dumbledore prioritized Snape in his plans as opposed to using Snape dangerously to give Harry an edge.

Eleanor Harrison-Dengate; "Dumbledore and Churchill: War Heroes of 1945"
http://www.mugglenet.com/2015/06/dumbledore-and-churchill-war-heroes-of-1945/
　　An interesting comparison of Albus Dumbledore to a real-life historical figure who may have served as an inspiration for him: Winston Churchill. This predated the renaissance of Churchill in popular culture, and remains a very good piece of analysis

HufflepuffSam; "The Master of Death"
http://www.mugglenet.com/2012/03/the-master-of-death/

One of the most recent pieces of relevant Potter scholarship, this essay examines what the concept of being Master of Death means and how no one ever achieved it in the HP series. Apart from anything else, there is the wonderful observation that the first time all three Hallows are united in one place is in a chapter titled (and all about) "Horcruxes," presaging the Hallows vs. Horcruxes debate.

Theowyn; "The Life and Lies of Albus Dumbledore"
http://www.the-leaky-cauldron.org/features/essays/issue21/lifeandliesalbusdumbledore/

Theowyn talks about Dumbledore manipulating things, much as this book does, but with the least charitable reading of Dumbledore I've found. Fans who are skeptical of Dumbledore's goodness and still have a hard time forgiving him will enjoy this one.

Sarah Putnam Park; "Dumbledorian Ethics"
http://www.the-leaky-cauldron.org/features/essays/issue21/dumbledorianethics/

In perhaps the most charitable reading of Dumbledore post-*Deathly Hallows*, Sarah argues that Dumbledore is really the Ultimate Utilitarian. It's worth reading in conjunction with Theowyn's to get both ends of the spectrum regarding Dumbledore.

Joyce Odell (a.k.a. Red Hen); "The Quirrell Debacle"
http://www.redhen-publications.com/quirrelldebacle.html

Red Hen (in her signature snippy tone) offers an alternate reading of *Sorcerer's Stone*, one where Quirrell is a victim whom Dumbledore is trying to rescue, and Harry is largely beside the point. Most interesting is a section near the end where Red Hen claims that Dumbledore was worried about Harry being like Tom Riddle and tested him with the Mirror of Erised.

D.W. Hill; "Snape and Dumbledore: The Unnecessary Bargain"
http://www.mugglenet.com/2007/11/snape-and-dumbledore-the-unnecessary-bargain/
   This piece was among the first to use the new information from *Deathly Hallows* to talk about the relationship between the Dumbledore and Snape, focusing specifically on Dumbledore's trust in Snape. My favorite bit is when Hill claims that Dumbledore trusts Snape because he relates to Snape's remorse over a loved one's death.

Avogadro; "Choice or Chance?"
http://www.the-leaky-cauldron.org/features/essays/issue19/choice/
   This essay, published very soon after *Deathly Hallows*, examined the worthwhile question of what ended up as the driving force in the final battle: choice or chance? That debate is a proxy to all that we've discussed here: how much of what happened was influenced by Dumbledore's efforts (choice), and how much of it happened regardless or despite his plans (chance)? Avogadro reaches a similar conclusion to me: it's both choice and chance working in conjunction that allow Harry to prevail.

Lady Lupin; Spinner's End #26: "Finite Incantatem"
http://www.mugglenet.com/2007/08/finite-incantatem/
   It has taken me a decade to puzzle all this out about Dumbledore, yet Lady Lupin arrived there exactly a month after *Deathly Hallows* was published. Her MuggleNet column, Spinner's End, correctly predicted more things in the last book than anyone

else's. This, her reaction piece to the last book, has a wonderful section on Albus, going over his motivations and his character in much the same way I did (though with fewer words). She, too, admires Dumbledore for his flaws and remains convinced he cared about Harry above all else.

Pre-*Deathly Hallows* Era

D.W. Hill; "Dumbledore's Trust in Snape Part 1: Headmaster and Schoolboy"
http://www.mugglenet.com/2007/06/dumbledores-trust-in-snape-part-1-headmaster-and-schoolboy/
    A month before *Deathly Hallows* was released, D.W. Hill wrote a wonderful trilogy of editorials titled Dumbledore's Trust in Snape. The publication of *Deathly Hallows* made much of it moot, but there are some excellent points in there.

D.W. Hill; "Dumbledore's Trust in Snape Part 2: More Than a Potions Master"
http://www.mugglenet.com/2007/06/dumbledores-trust-in-snape-part-2-more-than-a-potions-master/
    Hill makes the very intriguing claim that Snape is so nasty to Harry in order to get Harry emotional, allowing Snape to read his mind (on Dumbledore's orders).

D.W. Hill; "Dumbledore's Trust in Snape Part 3: Riffs and Curiosities"
http://www.mugglenet.com/2007/06/dumbledores-trust-in-snape-part-3-riffs-and-curiosities/
    Hill continues in the (rather charitable) vein that Snape is only being nasty for Harry's own good, and has some great insights into the end of *Prisoner of Azkaban* in particular.

D.W. Hill; "Severus Snape: A Portrait in Subtlety"
http://www.mugglenet.com/2007/03/severus-snape-a-portrait-in-subtlety/

    Hill wrote this essay in defense of Snape several months before *Deathly Hallows*, and there is an especially interesting section predicting that Snape is Dumbledore's Plan B for destroying the Horcruxes and so on.

Steve Connolly; "Dumbledore's Master Plan" (7 parts)
http://www.mugglenet.com/2007/03/dumbledores-master-plan-part-1/

    Steve Connolly essentially did what I attempted to do with this book—find Dumbledore's hand in all the events of the HP books—in a seven-part editorial (first part in the link). However, he does so several months before *Deathly Hallows* was published. To that end, the speculation in the first and last part largely proved to be inaccurate but is worth reading to see how intricately Rowling wove her tale. However, in the middle parts, Steve Connolly figures out many of the things I've written about, without the hindsight of *Deathly Hallows*! For example, in Part 6, he writes about how the prophecy is a decoy set up by Dumbledore.

Felicitys_mind; "Dumbledore's Boggart"
https://felicitys-mind.livejournal.com/3530.html

    This essay puts forward the theory that Dumbledore's boggart is harm coming to the children under his care, which is well-reasoned even if it turned out wrong. More interestingly, this piece brings forth the still valid theory that the potion in the cave that Dumbledore drank made him relive the torture of Amy Benson and Dennis Bishop.

Felicitys_mind; "Fantastic Potions and How They Helped Albus Dumbledore in HBP"
https://felicitys-mind.livejournal.com/2616.html

The first part of this essay builds on Cathy Leisner's "Stoppered Death Theory," which isn't available online. That theory accurately predicted that the curse on the Ringcrux was deadly and that Snape had "stoppered" Dumbledore's death (harkening back to Snape's speech in Harry's first Potions class). The Stoppered Death Theory successfully explained just about everything that went on in *Half-Blood Prince*. This essay then veers off into the theory that Dumbledore took Felix Felicis the night of his death, and how everything that happened actually helped him achieve his ultimate objectives.

Andrew Cooper; "Machiavelli's Half-Blood Prince"
http://www.the-leaky-cauldron.org/features/essays/issue9/machiavelli/

This is my favorite of the many essays written between HBP and DH about Snape being Machiavelli's Prince—it turned out very wrong but is no less clever for it.

B.J. Texan; "Machiavelli's Half-Blood Prince"
http://www.mugglenet.com/2006/04/machiavellis-half-blood-prince/

This is another essay marking Snape as Machiavelli's Prince, and claiming he would be the Big Bad of the series. However, there are a few extra gems in here. In particular, the essay correctly theorizes that Snape's Patronus is a big spoiler, though it guesses that the Patronus is a fox and therefore reveals the motif of The Prince.

Corinne Demyanovich & Michael Hagel; "Did Albus Dumbledore Set Up Events So That Harry Potter Would Go After the Philosopher's Stone?"
https://www.hp-lexicon.org/2006/01/21/did-albus-dumbledore-set-up-events-so-that-harry-potter-would-go-after-the-philosophers-stone/

    This is one of the earliest essays I found that really goes in-depth about Dumbledore orchestrating things in *Sorcerer's Stone*, and much of it is really spot-on.

Robbie Fischer; "He Did It All for Harry"
http://www.mugglenet.com/2006/01/the-burrow-he-did-it-all-for-harry/

    This was part of a series of eulogies for Dumbledore that MuggleNet hosted at The Burrow. Robbie raised the intriguing idea that Dumbledore gave Snape the D.A.D.A. position (which led to his own demise) purely to help Harry become an Auror.

Mudblood428; "Harry Says a Few Words"
http://www.mugglenet.com/2006/01/the-burrow-harry-says-a-few-words/

    In case there's been a little too much doom and gloom about Dumbledore, this essay (also part of the series of eulogies) is a good reminder of how much we (and Harry) loved Dumbledore.

DemenTom; "The New Ship at the Heart of Harry Potter"
http://www.mugglenet.com/2005/12/the-new-ship-at-the-heart-of-harry-potter/

    If you want a good laugh at how the fandom used to hero-worship Dumbledore, I think this essay is exemplary. Released in the half-year after *Half-Blood Prince* when we were all still processing our grief, this essay highlights everything from Dumbledore's politeness to his trust and belief in people.

WhiteAlchemist; "Kicking at Dumbledore's Corpse for Fun"
https://whitealchemist.livejournal.com/28846.html

This piece erroneously claims that Dumbledore was lying to Harry in HBP about who knows the contents of the prophecy. But it's notable as one of the first post-HBP pieces to seriously question Dumbledore's honesty while the rest of the fandom mourned him.

Daniela Teo; The Two-Way Mirror #22: "Love or Hate?"
http://www.mugglenet.com/2005/08/the-two-way-mirror-22-love-or-hate/

Less than a month after *Half-Blood Prince* came out, Daniela Teo at the Two-Way Mirror produced this fascinating take on Snape's relationship with Dumbledore. While missing the crucial fact of Dumbledore being in on the plan, she paints a compelling portrait of a Snape driven by resentment at Dumbledore due to Dumbledore's favoritism of Harry over Snape. It's also a welcome contrast to the exultation of Dumbledore taking place during that era.

Pre-*Half-Blood Prince* Era

Sophierom; "Dumbledore's Decisions and the Vulnerability of Authority"
https://hp-essays.livejournal.com/62338.html

Sophie wrote about the theme of hierarchical relationships versus equal ones in *Order of the Phoenix*. The theme is relevant to the entire series, and significant in this analysis because Dumbledore had no equals aside from Grindelwald.

Maline Fredén; The North Tower #35: "Albus Dumbledore—Clueless or Calculating"
http://www.mugglenet.com/2004/12/the-north-tower-albus-dumbledore-%C2%96-clueless-or-calculating/

The North Tower was one of the best regular columns on MuggleNet in its heyday, which is saying something. This essay discusses Dumbledore planning the events in *Sorcerer's Stone* and *Chamber of Secrets* much as I do, but without the benefit of having read the last two books. My favorite part is Maline's point that both Voldemort and Dumbledore have a weakness for wanting to win in a specific way.

Daniela Teo; The Two-Way Mirror #9: "Dumbledore's Plan"
http://www.mugglenet.com/2004/12/the-two-way-mirror-9-dumbledores-plan/

Prepare to be awed as you read this editorial. In MuggleNet's heyday, the columnists and editorialists would regularly build upon each other's writing, creating the kind of literary dialogue English professors can only dream of. Daniela built upon the above editorial by Maline and wrote this gem. It suggests that Dumbledore was willing to do some pretty morally questionable things in the service of his grand plan and suggests that Dumbledore actually planned Lily's sacrifice as part of his plan.

Although the particulars are wrong, keep in mind this was written in 2004. 2004, several years before *Deathly Hallows* proved her to be right on the money regarding Dumbledore's character! Aside from the very early predictions that Dumbledore would turn out to be the Big Bad of the series, this was one of the first essays to question Dumbledore's goodness, and almost certainly the first to get it right.

MarinaRusalka; "Thoughts on Dumbledore"
https://hp-essays.livejournal.com/6158.html
    This was written shortly after *Order of the Phoenix*, and holds up all these years later as one of the most damning indictments of Dumbledore's character I've ever read. Armed with only the first five books, Rusalka presciently paints a Dumbledore who is a master manipulator obsessed with others' loyalty to himself.

    For your convenience in following the links, this entire section is available at the book's website: LifeAndLiesOfDumbledore.com

Editions of the Potter books used in this volume:

J.K. Rowling, *Harry Potter and the Chamber of Secrets* (New York: Scholastic Inc, 2000)

J.K. Rowling, *Harry Potter and the Deathly Hallows* (New York: Scholastic Inc, 2009)

J.K. Rowling, *Harry Potter and the Goblet of Fire* (New York: Scholastic Inc, 2002)

J.K. Rowling, *Harry Potter and the Half-Blood Prince* (New York: Scholastic Inc, 2006)

J.K. Rowling, *Harry Potter and the Order of the Phoenix* (New York: Scholastic Inc, 2004)

J.K. Rowling, *Harry Potter and the Prisoner of Azkaban* (New York: Scholastic Inc, 2001)

J.K. Rowling, *Harry Potter and the Sorcerer's Stone* (New York: Scholastic Inc, 1999)

Acknowledgments

This book would not exist without a million things going right, and a million kindnesses (big and small) from too many people to mention. So before diving in, I offer a blanket "thank you" to everyone who ever did me a kindness—I assure you that, with my memory like a steel trap, I remember it and appreciate it.
Thanks to the team at Story Spring Publishing, the formidable Annie Tarbuck and Chris Hagberg, who did a terrific job editing this book into something I'm proud of. I'm so glad we worked together to publish the first edition of this book! Thank you for taking a chance on a hyper twenty-four-year-old crazy enough to think he could write a book—I have enjoyed every minute of debating with you about footnotes and abbreviations and hope I have at least slightly ameliorated your feelings towards Albus.

Thanks to Lorrie Kim, who paved the way for this book with *SNAPE*, and who talked me off a ledge many a time throughout this nerve-wracking publishing process. We may not agree on anything in the Potter series, but I hope we never stop arguing about it!

Thanks to Nancy Pina, without whom I never would have gotten this published. When I was recently out of college and broke, I was able to attend Leviosa 2016 only because you let me stay in your hotel room for free. That convention was where I met Annie and began the long road to publication, so this book would not be published without your generosity.

Thanks to Sheila Simmons, who designed an absolutely gorgeous cover for me. You made me finally understand the impulse to show people baby photos, because I accosted everyone I spoke to in the last year to show them your Dumbledorean masterpiece.

Thank you to the incredible team at Books of Wonder, my favorite bookstore, for taking a chance on me and my book. Thank you for allowing me to realize my dream of having a launch party at your store, for indulging my crazy choices like having a dance number at said launch party, and for not chasing me out when I was still signing books two hours after closing time.

Thanks to friends who lent their singing/dancing/baking/prophesying talents to my launch party: Deanna Benfante, Angelica Capotorto, dyAnne Irby, Mary Mandzak, Ignacio Melgar, Julie Stevens. And thanks to Caitlin Bryson and Angelica for helping with all the logistics of the launch party. I would have completely lost my mind without all of you; you really made sure my special day went off without a hitch.

Before my writings about Dumbledore were a book, they were a series of essays at MuggleNet, where I have been proudly publishing essays since 2011. Without that foundation, there would be no book here. Thanks to Kat Miller and the entire MuggleNet family—I'm sure I create a lot of work for you, both in terms of getting the essays published and in putting out fires when people finally read them.

Most little kids idolize musicians or athletes. When I was a kid, my heroes were the columnists at MuggleNet. I wanted to be Daniela Teo, Lady Lupin, Maline Freden, Bob Sindeldecker, Brandon Ford, Christopher Stephen, Dan Hoppel, and Josh Smith when I grew up. So even though I haven't heard of any of them in a decade, I remain grateful to them for their columns, and always try to hold myself to the high standard they set.

At nineteen, my dream came true when Noah Fried, the leader of MuggleNet's foundering Editorials section, offered me my own column at MuggleNet.

Noah, you were the one who first provided me with a platform to write about Dumbledore, and I hope you know what writing The Three Broomsticks has meant to me all these years. Thanks for that, and for all you put up with after branding me the "controversial columnist."

Thanks to the many and varied members of The Group That Shall Not Be Named—since our group is over 3,000 members strong, it would take too long to list everyone. But for ten years, you all have talked Potter with me, indulged my theorizing, and supported every crazy endeavor I've undertaken. Thanks for believing in my weirdness.

Thanks to Traci Hall, who allowed me to deliver presentations about Dumbledore at every MISTI-Con—I can hardly express how helpful these were in eventually crafting this book.

Thanks to Natasha Povar, Cherie Wong, Regina Burd, and all my oldest friends for their countless years of support. You're the ones who read my teenage memoirs and sappy poetry, and all those hours on the phone with you are the only thing that's kept me sane all these years.

Thanks to all the employers who wouldn't hire me in the fall of 2016—being unemployed for six months allowed me to realize my dream of completing a book, so I'm very glad I didn't go to work for you!

Lastly, thanks to Jo Rowling. The world that sprang from her imagination has shaped my life ever since I was nine years old, and I can't even fathom what my life would look like without Harry in it. Even as a published author, I am not up to the task of expressing what Harry Potter has meant to me. So I'll defer (as I often do) to wizard rock: "Thank you, Ms. J.K. Rowling... thank you so much for Harry."

About the Author

Attractive brunette Irvin Khaytman, twenty-six, whose savage quill has punctured many inflated reputations—

Never mind all that. Irvin Khaytman is a walking Harry Potter encyclopedia from New York City, where he does taxes by day and all things geeky by night. He has been writing essays about Harry Potter since 2007 as "hpboy13," and became a columnist at MuggleNet in 2011. In the last few years, he has also been a regular contributor to Hypable. When not reading or discussing books, Irvin can be found dancing to wizard rock or planning costumes for conventions. He identifies as a Ravenpuff.

Photo by G.M. Courtemanche

Lightning Source UK Ltd.
Milton Keynes UK
UKHW021927251119
354215UK00017BA/560/P